THE
HEROIC ENTHUSIASTS

(GLI EROICI FURORI)

GIORDANO BRUNO
translated by L. WILLIAMS

WITH AN INTRODUCTION, COMPILED CHIEFLY FROM DAVID LEVI'S "GIORDANO BRUNO O LA RELIGIONE DEL PENSIERO"

THE HEROIC ENTHUSIASTS

(*GLI EROICI FURORI*)

An Ethical Poem

By GIORDANO BRUNO

PART THE FIRST

PREFACE.

WHEN this Translation was begun, more than two years ago, for my own pleasure, in leisure hours, I had no knowledge of the difficulty I should find in the work, nor any thought of ever having it printed; but as "Gli Eroici Furori" of Giordano Bruno has never appeared in English, I decided to publish that portion of it which I have finished.

I wish to thank those friends who have so kindly looked over my work from time to time, and given me their help in the choice of words and phrases. I must, moreover, confess that I am keenly alive to the shortcomings and defects of this Translation.

I have used the word "Enthusiasts" in the title, rather than "Enthusiasms," because it seemed tome more appropriate.

L. W.FOLKESTONE,
September 1887.

INTRODUCTION.

NOLA, a city founded by the Chalcidian Greeks, at a short distance from Naples and from Vesuvius, was the birthplace of Giordano Bruno. It is described by David Levi as a city which from ancient times had always been consecrated to science and letters. From the time of the Romans to that of the Barbarians and of the Middle Ages, Nola was conspicuous for culture and refinement, and its inhabitants were in all times remarkable for their courteous manners, for valour, and for keenness of perception. They were, moreover, distinguished by their love for and study of philosophy; so that this city was ever a favourite dwelling-place for the choice spirits of the Renaissance. It may also be asserted that Nola was the only city of Magna Græcia which, in spite of the persecutions of Pagan emperors and Christian princes and clergy, always preserved the philosophical traditions of the Pythagoreans, and never was the sacred fire on the altar of Vesta suffered to become entirely extinct. Such was the intellectual and moral atmosphere in which Bruno passed his childhood. His paternal home was situated at the foot of Mount Cicada, celebrated for its fruitful soil. From early youth his pleasure was to pass the night out on the mountain, now watching the stars, now contemplating the arid, desolate sides of Vesuvius. He tells how, in recalling those days--the only peaceful ones of his life-he used to think, as he looked up at the infinite expanse of heaven and the confines of the horizon, with the towering volcano, that this must be the ultimate end of the earth, and it appeared as if neither tree nor grass refreshed the dreary space which stretched out to the foot of the bare smoky mountain. When, grown older, he came nearer to it, and saw the mountain so different from what it had appeared, and the intervening space that, seen from afar, had looked so bare and sterile, all covered with fruit-trees and enriched with vineyards, he began to see how illusory the judgment of the senses may be; and the first doubt was planted in his young soul as he perceived that, while the mind may grasp Nature in her grandeur and majesty, the work of the sage must be to examine her in detail, and penetrate to the cause of things.

When he appeared before the tribunal of the Holy Office at Venice, being asked to declare who and what he was, he said: "My name is Giordano, of the family of Bruno, of the city of Nola, twelve miles from Naples. There was I born and brought up. My profession has been and is that of letters, and of all the sciences. My father's name was Giovanni, and my mother was Francesca Savolini; and my father was a soldier. He is dead, and also mother. I am forty-four years old, having been born in 1548." He always regarded Nola with patriotic pride, and he received his first instruction in his father's house and in the public schools. Of a sad disposition, and gifted with a most lively imagination, he was from his earliest years given to meditation and to poetry. The, early years of Bruno's life were times of agitation and misfortune, and not propitious to study. The, Neapolitan provinces were disturbed by constant earthquakes, and devastated by pestilence and famine. The Turks fought, and ravaged the country, and made slaves of the inhabitants; the neighbouring provinces were still more harassed by hordes of bandits and outlaws, who invested Calabria, led by a terrible chief called Marcone. The Inquisition stood prepared to light its fires and slaughter the heretic. The Waldensians, who had lately been driven out of Piedmont, and had sought a shelter in the Calabrian territory were hunted down and given over to the executioner.

The convent was the only refuge from violence, and Bruno, either from religions enthusiasm, or in order to be able to devote himself to study, became a friar at the age of fifteen. There, in the quiet cloister of the convent of St. Dominic at Naples, his mind was nourished and his intellect developed; the cloistral and monkish education failed to enslave his: thought, and he emerged from this tutelage the boldest and least fettered of philosophers. Everything about this church and this convent, famous as having been the abode of Thomas Aquinas, was calculated to fire the enthusiasm of Bruno's soul; the leisure and quiet, far from inducing habits of indolence, or the sterile practices of asceticism, were stimulants to austere study, and to the fervour of mystical speculations. Here he passed nearly thirteen years of early manhood, until his intellect strengthened by study he began to long for independence of thought, and becoming, as he said himself, solicitous about the food of the soul and the culture of the mind, he found it irksome to go through automatically the daily vulgar routine of the convent; the pure flame of an elevated religious feeling being kindled in his soul, he tried to evade the vain exercises of the monks, the puerile gymnastics, and the adoration of so-called relics. His character was frank and open, and he was unable to hide his convictions; he put some of his doubts before his companions, and these hastened to refer them to the superiors; and thus was material found to institute a cause against him. It became known that he had praised the methods used by the Arians or Unitarians in expounding their doctrines, adding that they refer all things to the ultimate cause, which is the Father: this, with other heretical propositions, being brought to the notice of the Holy Office, Bruno found himself in the position of being first observed and then threatened. He was warned of the danger that hung over him by some friends, and decided to quit Naples. He fled from the convent, and took the road to Rome, and was there received in the monastery of the Minerva. A few days after his arrival in Rome he learned that instructions for his arrest had been forwarded from Naples; he tarried not, but got away secretly, throwing aside the monk's habiliments by the way. He wandered for some days about the Roman Campagna, his destitute condition proving a safeguard against, the bands of brigands that infested those lands, until,, arriving near Civita Vecchia, he was taken on board a Genoese vessel, and carried to the Ligurian port, where he hoped to find a, refuge from his enemies; but the city of Genova was devastated by pestilence and civil war, and after a sojourn of a few days he pursued once more the road of exile. Seeking for a place wherein he might settle for a short time and hide from his pursuers, he stayed his steps at Noli, situated at a short distance. from Savona, on the Riviera: this town, nestled in a little bay surrounded by high hills crowned by feudal castles and towers, was only accessible on the shore side, and offered a grateful retreat to our philosopher. At Noli, Bruno, obtained permission of the magistracy to teach grammar to children, and thus secured the means. of subsistence by the small remuneration he received; but this modest employment did not occupy him sufficiently, and he gathered round him a few gentlemen of the district, to whom he taught the science of the Sphere. Bruno also wrote a book upon the Sphere, which was lost. He expounded the system of Copernicus, and talked to his pupils with enthusiasm about the movement of the earth and of the plurality of worlds.

As in that same Liguria Columbus first divined another hemisphere outside the Pillars of Hercules, so Bruno discovered to those astonished minds the, myriads of worlds which fill the immensity of space. Columbus was derided and banished by his fellow-citizens, and the fate of our philosopher was similar to his. In the humble schoolmaster who taught grammar to the children, the bishop, the clergy, and the nobles, who listened eagerly to his lectures on the Sphere, began to suspect the heretic and the innovator. After five months it behoved him to leave Noli; he took the road to Savona, crossed the Apennines, and arrived at Turin. In Turin at that time reigned the great Duke Emanuele Filiberto, a man of strong character--one of those men who know how to found a dynasty and to fix the destiny of a people; at that time, when Central and Southern Italy were languishing under home and foreign tyranny, he laid the foundations of the future Italy.

He was warrior, artist, mechanic, and scholar. Intrepid on the field of battle, he would retire from deeds of arms to the silence of his study, and cause the works of Aristotle to be read to him; he spoke all the European languages; he worked at artillery, at models of fortresses, and at the smith's craft; he brought together around him, from all sides of Italy, artisans and scientists to promote industry, commerce, and science; he gathered together in Piedmont the most excellent compositors of Italy, and sanctioned a printer's company.

Bruno, attracted to Turin by the favour that was shown to letters and philosophy, hoped to get occupation as press reader; but it was precisely at that time that the Duke, instigated by France, was combating, with every kind of weapon, the Waldensian and Huguenot heresies, and had invited the Jesuits to Turin, offering them a substantial subsidy; so that on Bruno's arrival he found the place he had hoped for, as teacher in the, university, occupied by his enemies, and he therefore moved on with little delay, and embarked for Venice.

Berti, in his Life of Bruno, remarks that when the latter sought refuge in Turin, Torquato Tasso, also driven by adverse fortune, arrived in the same place, and he notes the affinity between them--both so great, both subject to every species of misfortune and persecution in life, and destined to immortal honours after their death: the light of genius burned in them both, the fire of enthusiasm flamed in each alike, and on the forehead of each one was set the sign of sorrow and of pain.

Both Bruno and Tasso entered the cloisters as boys: the one joined the Dominicans, the other the Jesuits; and in the souls of both might be discerned the impress of the Order to which they belonged. Both went forth from their native place longing to find a broader field of action. and greater scope for their intellectual powers. The one left Naples carrying in his heart the Pagan and Christian traditions of the noble enterprises and the saintly heroism of Olympus and of Calvary, of Homer and the Fathers, of Plato and St. Ignatius; the other was filled with the, philosophical thought of the primitive, Italian and Pythagorean epochs, fecundated by his own conceptions and by the new age; philosopher and apostle of an idea, Bruno consecrated his life to the development of it in his writings and to the propagation of his principles in Europe by the fire of enthusiasm. The one surprised the world with the melody of his songs; being, as Dante says, the "dolce sirena che i marinari in mezzo al mare smaga," he lulled the anguish that lacerated Italy, and gilded the chains which bound her; the other tried to shake her; to recall her to life with the vigour of thought, with the force of reason, with the sacrifice of himself. The songs of Tasso were heard and sung from one end of Italy to the other, and the poet dwelt in palaces and received the caress and smile of princes; while Bruno, discoursing in the name of reason and of science, was rejected, persecuted, and scourged, and only after three centuries of ingratitude, of calumny, and of forgetfulness, does his country show signs of appreciating him and of doing justice to his memory. In Tasso the poet predominates over the philosopher, in Bruno the philosopher predominates over and eclipses the poet. The first sacrifices thought to form; the second is careful only of the idea. Again, both are full of a conception of the. Divine, but the God that the dying Tasso confessed is a god that is expected and comes not; while the god that Bruno proclaims he already finds within himself. Tasso died in his bed in the cloister, uneasy as on a bed of thorns; Bruno, amidst the flames, stands out as on a pedestal, and dies serene and calm. We must now follow our fugitive to Venice.

At the time Giordano Bruno arrived in Venice that city was the, most important typographical centre of Europe; the commerce in books extended through the Levant, Germany, and France, and the. philosopher hoped that here he might find some means of subsistence. The plague at that time was devastating Venice, and in less than one year had claimed forty-two thousand victims; but Bruno felt no fear, and he took a lodging in that part or Venice called the Frezzeria, and was soon busy preparing for the press a work called "Segni del Tempo," hoping that the sale of it would bring a little money for daily needs. This work was lost, as were all those which he published in Italy, and which it was to the interest of Rome to destroy. Disappointed at not finding work to do in Venice, he next went to Padua, which was the intellectual centre of Europe, as Venice was the, centre of printing and publishing; the most celebrated professors of that epoch were to be found in the University of Padua, but at the time of Bruno's sojourn there, Padua, like, Venice, was ravaged by the plague; the university was closed, and the printing-house was not in operation. He remained there only a few days, lodging with some monks of the Order of St. Dominic, who, he relates, "persuaded me to wear the dress again, even though I would not profess the religion it implied, because they said it would aid me in my wayfaring to be thus attired; and so I got a white cloth robe, and I put on the hood which I had preserved when I left Rome." Thus habited he wandered for several months about the cities of Venetia and Lombardy, and although he contrived for a time to evade his persecutors, he finally decided to leave Italy, as it was repugnant to his disposition to live in forced dissimulation, and he felt that he could do no good either for himself or for his country, which was then overrun with Spaniards and scourged by petty tyrants; and with the lower orders sunk in ignorance, and the upper classes illiterate, uncultivated, and corrupt, the, mission of Giordano Bruno was impossible. "Altiora, Peto" was Bruno's motto, and to realize it he had gone forth with the pilgrim's staff in his hand, sometimes covered with the cowl of the monk, at others wearing the simple habit of a schoolmaster, or, again, clothed with the doublet of the mechanic he had found no resting-place--nowhere to lay his head, no one who could understand him, but always many ready to denounce him. He turned his back at last on his country, crossed the Alps on foot, and directed his steps towards Switzerland. He visited the universities in different towns of Switzerland, France, and Germany, and wherever he went he left behind him traces of his visit in some hurried writings. The only work of the Nolan, written in Italy, which as survived is "Il Candelajo," which was published in Paris. Levi, in his Life of Bruno, passes in review his various works; but it will suffice, here to reproduce what he says of the "Eroici Furori" the first part of which I have translated, and to note his remarks upon the style of Bruno, which presents many difficulties to the translator on account of its formlessness. Goethe says of Bruno's writings "Zu allgemeiner Betrachtung und Erhebung der Geistes eigneten sich die Schriften des Jordanus Brunous von Nola; aber freilich das gediegene Gold and Silber aus der Masse jener zo ungleich begabten Erzgänge auszuscheiden und unter den Hammer zu bringen erfordert fast mehr als menschliche Kräfte vermögen."'

I believe that no translation of Giordano Bruno's works has ever been brought out in English, or, at any rate, no translation of the "Eroici Furori," and therefore I have had no help from previous renderings. I have, for the most part, followed the text as closely as possible, especially in the sonnets, which are frequently rendered line for line. Form is lacking in the original, and would, owing to the unusual and often fantastic clothing of the ideas, be difficult to apply in the translation. He seems to have written down his grand ideas hurriedly, and, as Levi says, probably intended to retouch the work before printing.

Following the order of Levi's Life of Bruno, we next find the fugitive at Geneva. He was hardly thirty-one, years old when he quitted his country and crossed the Alps, and his first stopping-place, was Chambery, where he was received in a convent of the Order of Predicatori; he proposed going on to Lyons, but being told by in Italian priest, whom he met there, that he was not likely to find countenance or support, either in the place he was in or in any other place, however far he might travel, he changed his course and made for Geneva.

The name of Giordano Bruno was not unknown to the Italian colony who had fled from papal persecution to this stronghold of religious reform. He went to lodge at an inn, and soon received visits from the Marchese di Vico Napoletano, Pietro Martire Veimigli, and other refugees, who welcomed him with affection, inquiring whether he intended to embrace the religion of Calvin, to which Bruno replied that he did not intend to make profession of that religion, as he did not know of what kind it was, and he only desired to live in Geneva in freedom. He was then advised to doff the Dominican habit, which he still wore; this he was quite willing to do, only he had no money to buy other clothing, and was forced to have some made of the cloth of his monkish robes, and his new friends presented him with a sword and a hat; they also procured some work for him in correcting press errors.

The term of Bruno's sojourn in Geneva seems doubtful, and the precise, nature of his employment when there is also uncertain; but his independent spirit brought him into dispute with the rigid Calvinists of that city, who preached and exacted a blind faith, absolute and compulsory. Bruno could not accept any of the existing positive religious; he professed the cult of philosophy and science, nor was his character of that mould that would have enabled him to hide his principles. It was made known to him that he must either adopt Calvinism or leave Geneva: he declined the former, and had no choice as to the latter, poor he had entered Geneva, and poor he left it, and now turned his steps towards France.

He reached Lyons, which was also at that time a city of refuge against religious persecutions, and he addressed himself to his compatriots, begging for work from the publishers, Aldo and Grifi; but not succeeding in gaining enough to enable him to subsist, after a few days he left, and went on his way to Toulouse, where there was a famous university; and having made acquaintance with several men of intellect, Bruno was invited to lecture on the Sphere, which he did, with various other subjects, for six months, when the chair of Philosophy becoming vacant, he took the degree of Doctor, and competed for it; and he continued for two years in that place, teaching the philosophy of Aristotle and of others. He took for the text of his lectures the treatise of Aristotle, "De Anima," and this gave him the opportunity of introducing and discussing the deepest questions--upon the Origin and Destiny of Humanity; The Soul, is it Matter or Spirit? Potentiality or Reality? Individual or Universal? Mortal or Eternal? Is Man alone gifted with Soul, or are all beings equally so? Bruno's system was in his mind complete and mature; he taught that everything in Nature has a soul, one universal mind, penetrates and moves all things; the world itself is a sacrum animal. Nothing is lost, but all transmutes and becomes. This vast field afforded him scope for teaching his doctrines upon the world, on the, movement of the earth, and on the universal soul. The novelty and boldness of his opinions roused the animosity of the clergy against him, and after living two years and six months at Toulouse, he felt it wise to retire, and leaving the capital of the, Languedoc, he set his face towards Paris.

The two books--the fruit of his lectures—which he published in Toulouse, "De Anima" and "De Clavis Magis," were lost.

The title, of Doctor, or as he said himself, "Maestro delle Arti," which Bruno had obtained at Toulouse, gave him the faculty of teaching publicly in Paris, and he says "I went to Paris, where I set myself to read a most unusual lecture, in order to make myself known and to attract attention." He gave thirty lectures on the thirty Divine attributes, dividing and distributing them according to the method of St. Thomas Aquinas: these lectures excited much attention amongst the scholars of the Sorbonne, who went in crowds to hear him; and he introduced, as usual, his own ideas while apparently teaching the doctrines of St. Thomas. His extraordinary memory and his eloquence caused great astonishment; and the fame of Bruno reached the ears of King Henry III., who sent for him to the Court, and being filled with admiration of his learning, he offered him a substantial subsidy.

During his stay at Paris, although he was much at Court, he spent many hours in his study, writing the works that he afterwards published.

Philosophical questions were discussed at the Sobonne with much freedom: Bruno showed himself no partisan of either the Platonic or the Peripatetic school; he was not exclusive either in philosophy or in religion; he did not favour the Huguenot faction more than the Catholic league; and precisely by reason of this independent attitude, which kept him free of the shackles of the sects, did he obtain the faculty of lecturing at the Sorbonne. Nor can we ascribe this aloofness to religious indifference, but to the fact that he sought for higher things and longed for nobler ones. The humiliating spectacle which the positive religions, both Catholic and Reformed, presented at that time--the hatreds, the civil wars, the assassinations which they Instigated--had disgusted men of noble mould, and had turned them against these so-called religions; so that in Naples, in Tuscany, in Venice, in Switzerland, France, and England, there were to be found societies of philosophers, of free-thinkers, and politicians, who repudiated every positive religion and professed a pure Theism.

In the "Spaccio della Bestia Trionfante" he declares that he cannot ally himself either to the Catholic or the Lutheran Church, because he professes a more pure and complete faith than these--to wit, the love of humanity and the love of wisdom; and Mocenigo, the disciple who ultimately betrayed and sold him to the Holy Office, declares in his deposition that Bruno sought to make himself the author of a new religion under the name of "Philosophy." He was not a man to conceal his ideas, and in the fervour of his improvisation he no doubt revealed what he was; some tumult resulted from this free speaking of Bruno's, and he was forced to discontinue his lectures at the Sorbonne.

Towards the end of the year 1583 the King became enthralled by religious enthusiasm, and nothing was talked of in Paris but the conversion of King Henry. This fact changed the aspect of affairs as far as Bruno was concerned; he judged it prudent to leave Paris, and he travelled to England.

The principal works published by Bruno during his stay in Paris are "Il Candelajo" and "Umbrae Idearum." The former, says Levi, is a work of criticism and of demolition; in this comedy he sets in groups the principal types of hypocrisy, stupidity, and rascality, and exhibiting them in their true colours, he lashes them with ridicule. In the "Umbrae Idearum" he initiates the work of reconstruction, giving colour to his thought and sketching his idea. The philosophy of Bruno is based upon that of Pythagoras, whose system penetrates the social and intellectual history of Italy, both ancient and modern. The method of Pythagoras is not confined, as most philosophies are, to pure metaphysical speculations, but connects these with scientific observations and social practice. Bruno having resuscitated these doctrines, stamps them with a wider scope, giving them a more positive direction; and he may with propriety he called the second Pythagoras. The primal idea of Pythagoras, which Bruno worked out to a more distinct development is this: numbers are the beginning of things; in other words numbers are the cause of the existence of material things; they are not final, but are always changing position and attributes; they are variable and relative. Beyond and above this mutability there must be the Immutable, the All, the One.

The Infinite must be one, as one is the absolute number; in the original One is contained all the numbers; in the One is contained all the elements of the Universe.

This abstract doctrine required to be elucidated and fixed. From a hypothesis to concentrate and reduce it to a reality was the great work of Bruno.

One is the perfect number; it is the primitive monad. As from the One proceeds the infinite, series of numbers which again withdraw and are resolved into the One; so from Substance, which is one, proceed the myriads of worlds; from the worlds proceed myriads of living creatures; and from the union of one with the diverse is generated the Universe. Hence the progression from ascent to descent, from spirit to that which we call matter; from the cause to the origin, and the process of metaphysics, which, from the finite world of sense rises to the intelligent, passing through the intermediate numbers of infinite substance to active being and cosmic reason.

From the absolute One, the sun of the sensible and intellectual world, millions of stars and suns are produced or developed. Each sun is the centre of as many worlds which are distributed in as many distinct series in an infinite number of concentric and systems. Each system is attracted, repelled, and moved by an infinite, internal passion, or attraction; each turns round its own centre, and moves in a spiral towards the centre of the whole, towards which centre they all tend with infinite passional ardour. For in this centre, resides the sun of suns, the unity of unities, the temple, the altar of the universe, the sacred fire of Vesta, the vital principle of the universe.

That which occurs in the world off stars is reflected in the telluric world; everything has its centre, towards which it is attracted with fervour. All is thought, passion, and aspiration.

From this unity, which governs variety, from the movement of every world around its sun, of every sun around its centre sun--the sun of suns--which informs all with the rays of the spirit, with the light of thought--is generated that perfect harmony of colours, sounds, forms, which strike the sight and captivate and enthrall the intellect. That which in the heavens is harmony becomes, in the individual, morality, and in companies of human beings, law. That which is light in the spheres becomes intelligence and science in the world of the spirit and in humanity. We must study this harmony that rules the celestial worlds in order to deduce the laws which should govern civil bodies.

In the science of numbers dwells harmony, and therefore it behoves us to identify ourselves with this harmony, because from it is derived the harmonic law which draws men together into companies. Through the revolution of the worlds through space around their suns, from their order, their constancy and their measure, the mind comprehends the progress and conditions of men, and their duties towards each other. The Bible, the sacred book of man, is in the heavens; there does man find written the word of God.

Human souls are lights, distinct from the universal soul, which is diffused over all and penetrates everything. A purifying process guides them from one existence to another, from one form to another, from one world to another. The life of man is more than an experience or trial; it is an effort, a struggle to reproduce and represent upon earth some of that goodness, beauty, and truth which are diffused over the universe and constitute its harmony.

Long, slow, and full of opposition is this educational process of the soul. As the terraqueous globe becomes formed, changed, and perfected, little by little, through the cataclysms and convulsions which, by means of fire, flood, earthquake, and irruptions, transform the earth, so it is with humanity. Through struggle is man educated, fortified, and raised.

In the midst of social cataclysms and revolutions humanity has one guiding star, a beacon which shows its light above the storms and tempests, a mystical thread running through the labyrinth of history--namely, the religion of philosophy and of thought. The vulgar creeds would not, and have not dared to reveal the Truth in its purity and essence. They covered it with veils with allegories, with myths and mysteries, which they called sacred; they enshrouded thought with a double veil, and called it Revelation. Humanity, deceived by a seductive form, adored the veil, but did not lift itself up to the idea behind it; it saw the shadow, not the light.

But we must return to our wandering hero.

Bruno was about thirty-six years old when he left Paris and went to England. He was invited to visit the University of Oxford, and opened his lectures there with two subjects which, apparently diverse, are in reality intimately connected with each other--namely, on the Quadruple Sphere and on the Immortality of the Soul. Speaking of the immortality of the soul, he maintained that nothing in the universe is lost, everything changes and is transformed; therefore, soul and body, spirit and matter, are equally immortal. The body dissolves, and is transformed; the soul transmigrates, and, drawing round itself atom to atom, it reconstructs for itself a new body. The spirit that animates and moves all things is one; everything differentiates according to the different forms and bodies in which it operates. Hence, of animate things some are inferior by reason of the meanness of the organ in which they operate; others are, superior through the richness of the same. Thus we see that Bruno anticipates the doctrine, proclaimed later by Goethe and by Darwin, of the transformation of species and of the organic unity of the animal world; and this alternation from segregation to aggregation, which we call death and life, is no other than mutation of form.

After having criticised and scourged the religions of chimera, of ignorance, and hypocrisy, in "Lo Spaccio della Bestia Trionfante" and in "L'Asino Cillenico," the author, in "Gli Eroici Furori," lays down the basis for the religion of thought and of science. In place of the so-called Christian perfections (resignation, devotion, and ignorance), Bruno would put intelligence and the progress of the intellect in the world of physics, metaphysics, and morals; the true aim being illumination, the true morality the practice of justice, the true redemption the liberation of the soul from error, its elevation and union with God upon the wings of thought. This idea is developed in the work in question, which is dedicated to Sir Philip Sidney. After treating of the infinite universe, and contemplating the innumerable worlds in other works, he comes, in "Gli Eroici Furori," to the consideration of virtue in the individual, and demonstrates the potency of the human faculties. After the Cosmos, the Microcosm; after the infinitely great, the infinitely small. The body is in the soul, the soul is in the mind, the mind is in God. The life of the soul is the true life of the man. Of all his various faculties, that which rules all, that which exalts our nature, is Thought. By means of it we rise to the contemplation of the universe, and becoming in our turn creators, we raise the edifice of science; through the intellect the affections become purified, the will becomes strengthened. True liberty is acquired, and will and action becoming one through thought, we become heroes.

This education of the soul, or rather this elevation and glory of thought, which draws with it the will and the affections, not by means of blind faith or supernatural grace, not through an irrational and mystical impulse, but by the strength of a reformed intellect and by a palpable and well-considered enthusiasm, which science and the contemplation of Nature alone can give, this is the keynote of the poem. It is composed of two parts, each of which is divided into five dialogues: the first part, which may be called psychological, shows, by means of various figures and symbols drawn from Nature, how the divine light is always present to us, is inherent in man; it presents itself to the senses and to the comprehension: man constantly rejects and ignores it; sometimes the soul strives to rise up to it, and the poet describes the struggle with the opposing affections which are involved in this effort, and shows how at last the mail of intelligence overcomes these contending powers and fatal impulses which conflict within us, and by virtue of harmony and the fusion of the opposites the intellect becomes one with the affections, and man realizes the good and rises to the knowledge of the true. All conflicting desires being at last united, they become fixed upon one object, one great intent-- the love of the Divine, which is the highest truth and the highest good. In "Gli Eroici Furori" we see Bruno as a man, as a philosopher, and as a believer: here he reveals himself as the here of thought. Even as Christ was the hero of faith, and sacrificed himself for it, so Bruno declares himself ready to sacrifice himself for science. It is also a literary, a philosophical, and a, religious work; form, however, is sacrificed to the idea--so absorbed is the author in the idea that he often ignores form altogether. An exile wandering from place to place, he wrote hurriedly and seldom or ever had he the opportunity of revising what he had written down. His mind in the impulsiveness of its improvisation was like the volcano of his native soil, which, rent by subterranean flames, sends forth from its vortices of fire, at the same time smoke, ashes, turbid floods, stones, and lava. He contemplates the soul, and seeks to understand its language; he is a physiologist and a naturalist, merged in the mystic and the enlightened devotee.

Bruno might have made a fixed home for himself in England, as so many of his compatriots had done, and have continued to enjoy the society of such men as Sir Philip Sydney, Fulke Greville, and, perchance, also of Shakespeare himself, who was in London about that time; but his self-imposed mission allowed him no rest; he must go forth, and carry his doctrines to the world, and forget the pleasures of friendship and the ties of comfort in the larger love of humanity; his work was to awaken souls out of their lethargy, to inspire them with the love of the highest good and of truth; to teach that God is to be found in the study of Nature, that the laws of the visible world will explain those of the invisible, the union of science. and humanity with Nature and with God.

Bruno returned to Paris in 1585, being at that time tutor in the family of Manvissier, who had been recalled from England by his Sovereign. During Bruno's second sojourn in Paris efforts were made by Mendoza, the Spanish and others, to induce him to return to his allegiance to the Church, and to be reconciled to the Pope; but Bruno, declined these overtures, and soon after left Paris for Germany, where he arrived on foot his only burden being a few books.

He visited Marburg and Wurtemburg, remaining in the latter place two years, earning his bread by teaching.

Prague and Frankfort were next visited; ever the same courage and boldness characterized his teaching and ever the same scanty welcome was accorded to it, although in every city and university crowds of the intelligent listened to his lectures; but the Church never lost sight of Bruno, he was always under surveillance, and few dared to show themselves openly his friends. Absorbed in his studies and intent upon his work, writing with feverish haste, he observed nothing of the invisible net which his enemies kept spread about him, and while his slanderers were busy in doing him injury he was occupied in teaching the mnemonic art, and explaining his system of philosophy to the young Lutherans who attended his lectures; in settling the basis of a new and rational religion, and in writing Latin verses; using ever greater diligence with his work, almost as if he felt that, the time was drawing near in which he would be no longer at liberty to work and teach.

It was during the early part of the pontificate of Gregory XIV. that Bruno received letters from Mocenigo in Venice, urging him to return to Italy, and to go and stay with him in Venice, and instruct him in the secrets of science. Bruno was beginning to tire of this perpetually wandering life, and after several letters from Mocenigo, full of fine professions of friendship and protection, Bruno, longing to see his country again, turned his face towards Venice.

In those days men of superior intellect were often considered to be magicians or sorcerers; Mocenigo, after enticing Bruno to Venice, insisted upon his teaching him "the secret of memory and other things that he knew."

The philosopher with untiring patience tried to instil into this dull head the principles of logic, the elements of mathematics, and the rudiments of the mnemonic art; but the pupil hated study, and had no faculty of thought; yet he insisted that Bruno should make science clearly known to him! But this was probably only to initiate a quarrel with Bruno, whom he intended afterwards to betray, and deliver into the hands of the Church.

The Holy Office would have laid hands on Bruno immediately on his arrival in Italy, but being assured by Mocenigo that he could not escape, they left him a certain liberty, so that he might more surely compromise himself, while his enemies were busy collecting evidence against him. When at last his eyes became opened to what was going on about him, and he could no longer ignore the peril of his position, it was too late; Bruno could not get away, and was told by Mocenigo that if he stayed not by his own will and pleasure, he would be compelled to remain where he was. Bruno, however, made his preparations for departure, and sent his things on to Frankfort, intending to leave the next day himself; but in the, morning, while he was still in bed, Mocenigo entered the chamber, pretending that he wished to speak with him; then calling his servant Bartolo and five or six gondoliers, who waited without, they forced Bruno to rise, and conducted him to a garret, and locked him in. There he passed the first day of that imprisonment which was to last for eight years. The next day he went over the lagoon in a gondola, in the company of his Jailers, who took him to the prison of the Holy Office, and left him there. Levi devotes many pages to the accusations brought against Giordano Bruno by the Inquisitors, and the depositions and denunciations. made against him by his enemies. The Court was opened without delay, and most of the provinces of Italy were represented by their delegates in the early part of the trial; Bruno himself, being interrogated, gave ail account in detail of his life, of his wanderings, of his occupations and works: serene and dignified before this terrible tribunal, he expounded his doctrine, its principles, and logical consequences. He spoke of the universe, of the infinite, worlds in infinite space, of the divinity in all things, of the unity of all things, the dependence and inter-dependence of all things, and of the existence of God in all. After nine months' imprisonment in Venice, towards the end of January 1593, Bruno, in chains, was conveyed from the Bridge of Sighs through the lagoons to Ancona, where he remained incarcerated until the prison of the Roman Inquisition received him. If we look upon "Gli Eroici Farori" as a prophetical poem, we see that his sufferings in the loneliness of his prison--and in the torture-chamber of the Inquisition passed by anticipation before his mind in the book written when he was free and a wanderer in strange lands.

"By what condition, nature, or fell chance,
In living death, dead life I live?"

he writes eight years and more before he ever breathed the stifling air of a dungeon; and again:

The soul nor yields nor bends to these rough blows,
But bears, exulting, this long martyrdom,
And makes a harmony of these sharp pangs."

Further details of the trial of Giordano Bruno are to be found in Levi's book. It is well known how he received the sentence of death passed upon him, saying: "You, O judges! feel perchance more terror in pronouncing this judgment than I do in hearing it." The day fixed for the burning, which was to take place in the Campo dei Fiori, was the 17th February in the year 1600. Rome was full of pilgrims from all parts, come to celebrate the jubilee of Pope Clement VIII. Bruno was hardly fifty years old at this time; his face was thin and pale, with dark, fiery eyes; the forehead luminous with thought, his body frail and bearing the signs of torture; his hands in chains, his feet bare, he walked with slow steps in the early morning towards the funeral pile. Brightly shone the sun, and the flames leapt upwards and mingled with his ardent rays; Bruno stood in the midst with his arms crossed, his head raised, his eyes open; when all was consumed, a monk took a handful of the ashes and scattered them in the wind. A month later, the Bishop of Sidonia presented himself at the Treasury of the Pope, and demanded two scudi in payment for having degraded Fra Giordano the heretic.

"L'incendio è tal, ch'io m'ardo e non mi sfaccio."
EROICI FURORI.

THE HEROIC ENTHUSIASTS.

First Dialogue.

TANSILLO, CICADA.

TANS. The enthusiasms most suitable to be first brought forward and considered are those that I now place before you in the order that seems to me most fitting.

CIC. Begin, then, to read.

TANSILLO.

I. Ye Muses, that so oft I have repulsed,
That, now importuned, haste to cure my pain,
And to console me in my woes
With verses, rhymes, and exaltation
Such as to others ye did never show,
Who yet do vaunt themselves of laurel and of myrtle,
Be near me now, my anchor and my port,
Lest I for sport should towards some others turn.
O Mount! O Goddesses! O Fountain!
Where and with whom I dwell, converse and nourish me,
Where peacefully I ponder and grow fair;
I rise, I live: heart, spirit, brows adorn;
Death, cypresses, and hells
You change to life, to laurels, and eternal stars!

It is to be supposed that he oftimes and for divers reasons had repulsed the Muses; first, because he could not be idle as a priest of the Muses should be, for idleness cannot exist there, where the ministers and servants of envy, ignorance, and malignity are to be combated. Moreover, he could not force himself to the study of philosophies, which though they be not the most mature, yet ought, as kindred of the Muses, to precede them. Besides which, being drawn on one side by the tragic Melpomene, with more matter than spirit, and on the other side by the comic Thalia, with more spirit than matter, it came to pass that, oscillating between the two, he remained neutral and inactive, rather than operative. Finally, the dictum of the censors, who, restraining him from that which was high and worthy, and towards which he was naturally inclined, sought to enslave his genius, and from being free in virtue they would have rendered him contemptible under a most vile and stupid hypocrisy. At last, in the great whirl of annoyances by which he was surrounded, it happened that, not having wherewith to console him, he listened to those who are said to intoxicate him with such exaltation, verses, and rhymes, as they had never demonstrated to others; because this work shines more by its originality than by its conventionality.

CIC. Say, what do you mean by those who vaunt themselves of myrtle and laurel?

TANS. Those may and do boast of the myrtle who sing of love: if they bear themselves nobly, they may wear a crown of that plant consecrated to Venus, of which they know the potency. Those may boast of the laurel who sing worthily of things pertaining to heroes, substituting heroic souls for speculative and moral philosophy, and praising them and setting as mirrors and exemplars for political and civil actions.

CIC. There are then many species of poets and crowns?

TAM. Not only as many as there are Muses, but a great many more; for although genius is to be met with, yet certain modes and species of human ingenuity cannot be thus classified.

CIC. There are certain schoolmen who barely allow Homer to be a poet, and set down Virgil, Ovid, Martial, Hesiod, Lucretius, and many others as versifiers, judging them by the rules of poetry of Aristotle.

TANS. Know for certain, my brother, that such as these are beasts. They do not consider that those rules serve principally as a frame for the Homeric poetry, and for other similar to it, and they set up one as a great poet, high as Homer, and disallow those of other vein, and art, and enthusiasm, who in their various kinds are equal, similar, or greater.

CIC. So that Homer was not a poet who depended upon rules, but was the cause, of the rules which serve for those who are more apt at imitation than invention, and they have been used by him who, being no poet, yet knew how to take the rules of Homeric poetry into service, so as to become, not a poet or a Homer, but one who apes the Muse of others?

TANS. Thou dost well conclude that poetry is not born in rules, or only slightly and accidentally so; the rules are derived from the poetry, and there are as many kinds and sorts of true, rules as there are kinds and sorts of true poets.

CIC. How then are the true poets to be known?

TANS. By the singing of their verses; in that singing they give delight, or they edify, or they edify and delight together.

CIC. To whom then are the rules of Aristotle useful?

TANS. To him who, unlike Homer, Hesiod, Orpheus, and others, could not sing without the rules of Aristotle, and who, having no Muse of his own, would coquette with that of Homer.

CIC. Then they are wrong, those stupid pedants of our days, who exclude from the number of poets those who do not use words and metaphors conformable to, or whose principles are not in union with, those of Homer and Virgil; or because they do not observe the custom of invocation, or because they weave one history or tale with another, or because they finish the song with an epilogue on what has been said and a prelude on what is to be said, and many other kinds of criticism and censure, from whence it seems they would imply that they themselves, if the fancy took them, could be the true poets; and yet in fact they are no other than worms, that know not how to do anything well, but are born only to gnaw and befoul the studies and labours of others; and not being able to attain celebrity by their own virtue and ingenuity, seek to put themselves in the front, by hook or by crook, through the defects and errors of others.

TANS. Now, to return from this long digression, I say that there are as many sorts of poets as there are human sentiments and ideas; and to these it is possible to adapt garlands, not only of every species of plant, but also of other kinds of material. SO the crowns of poets are made not only of myrtle and of laurel, but of vine leaves for the white-wine verses, and of ivy for the bacchanals; of olive for sacrifice and laws; of poplar, of elm, and of corn for agriculture; of cypress for funerals, and innumerable others for other occasions; and, if it please you, also of that material signified by a good fellow when he exclaimed:

O Friar Leek! O Poetaster!
That in Milan didst buckle on thy wreath
Composed of salad, sausage, and the pepper-caster.

CIC. Now surely he of divers moods, which he exhibits in various ways, may cover himself with the branches of different plants, and may hold discourse worthily with the Muses, for they are his aura or comforter, his anchor or support, and his harbour, to which he retires in times of labour, of agitation, and storm. Hence he cries: "O mountain of Parnassus, where I abide! Muses, with whom I converse! Fountain of Helicon, where I am nourished. Mountain, that affordest me a quiet dwelling-place! Muses, that inspire me with profound doctrines. Fountain, that cleanses me! Mountain, on whose ascent my heart uprises! Muses, that in discourse revive my spirit. Well, whose arbours cool my brows! Change my death into life, my cypress to laurels, and my hells into heavens: that is, give me immortality, make me poet, render me illustrious!"

TANS. Well; because to those whom Heaven favours the greatest evils turn to greatest good, for needs or necessities bring forth labours and studies, and these most often bring the glory of immortal splendour.

CIC. For to die in one age makes us live in all the rest. Go on.

TANS. Then follows:

2. In form and place like to Parnassus is my heart,
And up unto this mount for safety I ascend;
My Muses are my thoughts, and they present to me
At every hour new beauties counted out.
The frequent tears that from my eyes do pour,

These make my fount of Helicon.
By such a mount, such nymphs, such floods,
As Heaven did please, was I a poet born.
No king of any kingdom,
No favouring hand of emperor,
No highest priest nor great pastòr,
Has given to me such graces, honours, privileges,
As are those laurel leaves with which
O'ershadowed are my heart, my thoughts, my tears.

Here he declares his mountain to be the exalted affection of his heart, his Muses he calls the beauties and attributes of the object of his affections, and the fountain is his tears. In that mountain affection is kindled; through those beauties enthusiasm is conceived, and by those tears the enthusiastic affection is demonstrated; and he esteems himself not less grandly crowned by his heart, his thoughts, and his tears than others are by the band of kings, emperors, and popes.

CIC. Explain to me what he means by his heart being in form like Parnassus.

TANS. Because the human heart has two summits, which terminate in one base or root; and, spiritually, from one affection of the heart proceed two opposites, love and hate; and the mountain of Parnassus has two summits and one base.

CIC. On to the next!

3. The captain calls his warriors to arms,
And at the trumpet's sound they all
Under one sign and standard come.
But yet for some in vain the call is heard,
Heedless and unprepared, they mind it not.
One foe he kills, and the insane
He banishes from out the camp in scorn.
And thus the soul, when foiled her high designs,
Would have all those opponents dead or gone;
One object only I regard,
One face alone my mind does fill,
One beauty keeps me fixed and still;
One arrow pierced my heart, and one
The fire with which alone I burn,
And towards one paradise I turn.

This captain is the human will, which dwells in the depths of the, soul with the small helm of reason to govern and guide the interior powers against the wave of natural impulses. He, with the sound of the trumpet--that is, by fixed resolve--calls all the warriors or invokes all the powers; called warriors because they are in continual strife and opposition; and their affections, which are all contrary thoughts, some towards one and some towards the other side inclining, and he tries to bring them all under one flag--one settled end and aim. Some are called in vain to put in a ready appearance, and are chiefly those which proceed from the lower instincts, and which obey the reason either not at all, or very little; and forcing himself to prevent their actions and condemn those which cannot be prevented, he shows himself as one who would kill those and banish these, now by the scourge of scorn, now by the sword of anger. One only is the object of his regards, and on this he is intently fixed; one prospect delights and fills his imagination, one beauty pleases, and he rests in that, because the operation of the intelligence is not a work of movement but of quiet; from thence alone he derives that barb which, killing him, constitutes the consummation of perfection. He burns with one fire alone; that is, one affection. consumes him.

CIC. Why is love symbolized by fire?

TANS. For many reasons, but at present let this one suffice thee: that as love converts the thing loved into the lover, so amongst the elements fire is active and potent to convert all the others, simple and composite, into itself.

CIC. Go on.

TANS. He knows one paradise--that is, one consummation, because paradise commonly signifies the end; which is again distinguished from that which is absolute in truth and essence from that which is so in appearance and shadow or form. Of the first there can only be one, as there can be only one ultimate and one primal good. Of the second the modes are infinite.

    4. Love, Fate, Love's object, and cold Jealousy,
    Delight me, and torment, content. me, and afflict.
    The insensate boy, the blind and sinister,
    The loftiest beauty, and my death alone

Show to me paradise, and take away.
Present me with all good, and steal it from me,
So that the heart, the mind, the spirit, and the soul,
Have joy, pain, cold, and weight in their control.
Who will deliver me from war?
Who give to me the fruit of love in peace?
And that which vexes that which pleases me
(Opening the gates of heaven and closing them)
Who will set far apart
To make acceptable my fires and tears?

He shows the reason and origin of passion; and whence it is conceived; and how enthusiasm is born, by ploughing the field of the Muses and scattering the seed of his thoughts and waiting for the fruitful harvest, discovering in himself the fervour of the affections instead of in the sun, and in place of the rain is the moisture of his eyes. He brings forward four things: Love, Fate, the Object, and Jealousy. Here love is not a low, ignoble, and unworthy motor, but a noble lord and chief. Fate is none other than the pre-ordained disposition and order of casualties to which he is subject by his destiny. The object is the thing loved and the correlative of the lover. Jealousy, it is clear, must be the ardour of the lover about the thing loved, of which it boots not to speak to him who knows what love is, and which it is vain to try to explain to others. Love delights, because to him who loves it is a pleasure to love; and he who really loves would not cease from loving. This is referred to in the following sonnet:

5. Beloved, sweet, and honourable wound,
From fairest dart that love did choose,
Lofty, most beauteous and potential zeal,
That makes the soul in its own flames find weal!
What power or spell of herb or magic art
Can tear thee from the centre of my heart,
Since he, who with an over growing zest,
Tormenting most, yet most does make me blest?
How can I of this weight unburdened be,
If pain the cure, and joy the sore give me?
Sweet is my pain: to this world new and rare.
Eyes! ye are the bow and torches of my lord!

Double the flames and arrows in my breast,
For languishing is sweet and burning best.

Fate vexes and grieves by undesirable and unfortunate events, or because it makes the subject feel unworthy of the object, and out of proportion with the dignity of the latter, or because a perfect sympathy does not exist, or for other reasons and obstacles that arise. The object satisfies the subject, which is nourished by no other, seeks no other, is. occupied by no other, and banishes every other thought. Jealousy torments, because although she is the daughter of Love, and is derived from him, and is his companion who always goes with him, and is a sign of the same, being understood as a necessary consequence wherever love is found (as may be observed of whole generations who, from the coldness of the region and lateness of development, learn little, love less, and of jealousy know nothing), yet, notwithstanding its kinship, association, and signification, jealousy comes to trouble and poisons all that it finds of beautiful and of good in Love. Therefore I said in another sonnet:

6. Oh, wicked child of Envy and of Love!
That turnest into pain thy father's joys,
To evil Argus-eyed, but blind as mole to good.
Minister of torment! Jealousy!
Fetid harpy! Tisiphone infernal!
Who steals and poisons others' good,
Under thy cruel breath does languish
The sweetest flower of all my hopes.
Proud of thyself, unlovely one,
Bird of sorrow and harbinger of ill,
The heart thou visitest by thousand doors;
If entrance unto thee could be denied,
The reign of Love would so much fairer be,
As would this world were death and hate away.

To the above is added, that Jealousy not only is sometimes the ruin and death of the lover, but often kills Love itself, because Love comes to be so much under its influence that it is impelled to despise the object, and in fact becomes alienated from it, especially when it engenders disdain.

CIC. Explain now the ideas which follow. Why is Love called the "insensate boy"?

TANS. I will tell you. Love is called the insensate boy, not because he is so of himself, but because he brings certain ones into subjection, and dwells in such subjects, since the more intellectual and speculative one is, the more Love raises the genius and purifies the intellect, rendering it alert, studious, and circumspect, promoting a condition of valorous animosity and an emulation of virtues and dignities by the desire to please and to make itself worthy of the thing loved; others, and they are the largest number, call him mad and foolish, because he drives them distracted, and hurries them into excesses, by which the spirit, soul, and body become sickly, and inept to consider and distinguish that which is seemly from that which is distorted; thus rendering them subject to scorn, derision, and reproach.

CIC. It is commonly said that love makes fools of the old and makes the young wise.

TANS. That drawback does not happen to all the aged, nor that advantage to all the young; the one is true of the weak, and the other of the robust. One thing is certain, that he who loves wisely in youth will in age not go astray. But derision is for those of mature age, into whose hands Love puts the alphabet.

CIC. Tell me now why Fate is called blind and bad.

TANS. Again, blind and bad is not said of Destiny itself, because it is of the same order and number and measure as the universe; but as to the subjects it is said to be blind, for they are, blind to fate, she being so uncertain. So also is Fate said to be evil, because every living mortal who laments and complains, blames her. As the Apulian poet says:

How is it, or what means it, Mæcenas,
That none on earth contented with that fate appear,
Which Reason or Heaven has assigned to them?

In the same way he calls the object the highest beauty, as it is that alone which has power of attracting him to itself; and this he holds it more worthy, more noble, and feels it predominant and superior as he becomes subject and captive to it. "My death itself," he says of Jealousy, because as Love has no more close companion than she, so also he feels he has no greater enemy; as nothing is more hurtful to iron than rust, which is produced by it.

CIC. Now, since you have begun so, continue to show bit by bit that which remains.

TANS. So will I. He says next of Love: he shows me Paradise, in order to prove that Love himself is not blind, and does not himself render any lovers blind, except through the ignoble characteristics of the subject; even as the birds of night become blind in the sunshine. As for himself, Love brightens, clears, and opens the intellect, permeating all and producing miraculous effects.

CIC. Much of this, it seems to me, the Nolano demonstrates in another sonnet:

7. Love, through whom high truth I do discern,
Thou openest the black diamond doors;
Through the eyes enters my deity, and through seeing
Is born, lives, is nourished, and has eternal reign;
Shows forth what heaven holds, earth and hell:
Makes present true images of the absent;
Gains strength: and drawing with straight aim,
Wounds, lays bare and frets the inmost heart.
Attend now, thou. base hind unto the truth,
Bend down the car to m unerring word;
Open, open, if thou canst the eyes, foolish perverted one!
Thou understanding little, call'st him child,
Because thou swiftly changest, fugitive he seems,
Thyself not seeing, call'st him blind.

Love shows Paradise in order that the highest things may be heard, understood, and accomplished; or it makes the things loved, grand-at least in appearance. He says, Fate takes love away; because, often in spite of the lover, it does not concede, and that which he sees and desires is distant and adverse to him. Every good he sets before me, he says of the object, because that which is indicated by the finger of Love seems to him the only thing, the principal, and the whole. "Steals it from me," he says of Jealousy, not simply in order that it may not be present to me; removing it from my eyesight, but in order that good may not be good, but an acute evil; sweet, not sweet, but an agonized longing; while the heart--that is, the will, has joy by the great force of love, whatever may be the result; the mind--that is, the intellectual part, has pain through the Fear of Fate, which fate does not favour the lover; the spirit--that is, the natural affections, are cold because they are snatched from the object which gives joy to the heart, and which might give pleasure to the mind; the soul--that is, the suffering and sensitive soul, is heavy--that is, finds itself oppressed with the heavy burden of jealousy which torments it. To this consideration of his state he adds a tearful lament, and says: "Who will deliver me from war, and give me peace? or who will separate that which pains and injures me from that which I so love, and which opens to me the gates of heaven, so that the fervid flames in my heart may be acceptable, and fortunate the fountains of my tears?" Continuing this proposition, he adds:

> 8. Ah me! oppress some other, spiteful Fate!
> Jealousy, get thee hence--begone! away!
> These may suffice to show me all the grace
> Of changeful Love, and of that noble face.
> He takes my life, she gives me death,
> She wings, he burns my heart,
> He murders it, and she revives the soul:
> My succour she, my grievous burden he!
> But what say I of Love?
> If he and she one subject be, or form,
> If with one empire and one rule they stamp
> One sole impression in my heart of hearts,
> Then are they two, yet one, on which do wait
> The mirth and melancholy of my state!

Four beginnings and extremes of two opposites he would reduce to two beginnings and one opposite: he says, then, oppress others--that is, let it suffice thee, O my Fate! that thou hast so much oppressed me; and since thou canst not exist without exercise of thyself, turn elsewhere thy anger. Get thee hence out of the world, thou Jealousy, because one of those two others which remain can supply your functions and offices; yet, O Fate! thou art none other than. my love; and thou, Jealousy, art not external to the substance of the same. He alone, then, remains; to deprive me of life, to burn me, to give me death, and to be to me the burden of my bones; for he delivers me from death--wings, enlivens, and sustains. Then two beginnings and one opposite he reduces to one beginning and one result, exclaiming But what do I say of Love? If this presence, this object, is his empire, and appears none other than the empire of Love, the rule of Love and its own rule; the impression of Love which appears in the substance of my heart, is then no other impression than its own, and therefore after having said "Noble face," replies "Inconstant Love."

Second Dialogue

TANSILLO.

Now begins the enthusiast to display the affections. and uncover the wounds which are for a sign in his body, and in substance or essence in his soul, and he says thus:

9. Of Love the standard-bearer I;
My hopes are ice, and glowing my desires.
At once I tremble, sparkle, freeze, and burn;
Am mute, and fill the air with clamorous plaints.
Water my eyes distil, sparks from my heart.
I live, I die, make merry and lament.
Living the waters, the burning never dies,
For in my eyes is Thetys, and Vulcan in my heart.
Others I love; myself I hate.
If I be winged, others are changed to stone;
They high as heaven, if I be lowly set.
I cease not to pursue, they ever flee away;
If I do call, yet none will answer me.
The more I search, the more is hid from me.

In accordance with this, I will continue with that which just before I said to thee, that one should not strive so hard to prove that which is so very evident-namely, that there is nothing pure and unalloyed; and some have said that no mixed thing is a real entity, as alloyed gold is not real gold, manufactured wine is not real simple wine. Almost all things are made up of opposites, whence it comes that the success of our affections, through the mixture that is in things, can afford no pleasure without some bitterness; and more than this, I will say, that were it not for the bitter, there would be no sweet; seeing that it is through fatigue that we find pleasure in repose; separation is the cause of our pleasure in union and, examining generally, we shall ever find that one opposite is the reason that the other opposite pleases and is desired.

CIC. Then there is no delight without the contrary?

TANS. Certainly not; as without the opposite there is no pain; as is shown by that golden Pythagorean poet when he says:

Hinc metuunt cupiuntque, dolent gaudentque, nec Respiciunt, clausæ tenebris, e carcere cæco.

This, then, is what the mixture of things causes, and hence it is that no one is pleased with his own state, except some senseless blockhead, who is so all the more the deeper is the degree of obscure folly in which he is sunk; then he has little or no apprehension of pain; he enjoys the actual present without fearing the future; he enjoys that which is and that in which he finds himself, and has neither care nor sorrow for what may be; and, in short, has no sense of that opposition which is symbolized by the tree of the knowledge of good and evil.

CIC. From this we see that ignorance is the mother of sensual felicity and beatitude, and this same is the garden of paradise of the animals; as is made clear in the dialogues of the Kabala of the horse Pegasus; and as says the wise Solomon, "Whose increases knowledge increases sorrow."

TANS. Hence it appears that heroic love is a torment, because it does not enjoy the present, as does animal love, but is of the future and the absent; and, on the contrary, it feels ambition, emulation, suspicion and dread. One evening, after supper, a certain neighbour of ours said: "Never was I more, jolly than I am now." John Bruno, father of the Nolano, answered him: "Never wert thou more foolish than now."

CIC. You would imply, then, that he who is sad is wise, and that other who is more sad is wiser?

TANS. On the contrary, I mean that there is in these another species of foolishness and a worse.

CIC. Who, then, is wise, if foolish is he who is content, and foolish he who is sad?

TANS. He who is neither merry nor sad.

CIC. Who? He who sleeps? He who is without feeling-- who is dead?

TANS. No; but he who is quick, both seeing and hearing, and who, considering evil and good, estimating the one and the other as variable, and consistent in motion, mutation, and vicissitude, in such wise that the end of one opposite is the commencement of another, and the extreme of the one is the beginning of the other; whose spirit is neither depressed nor elated, but is moderate in inclinations and temperate in desires; to him pleasure is not pleasure, having ever present the end of it; equally, pain to him is not pain, because by the force of reasoning he has present the end of that too. So the sage holds all mutable things as things that are not, and affirms that they are no other than vanity and nothingness, because time has to eternity the proportion of the point to the line.

CIC. So that we can never hold the proposition of being contented or discontented, without holding the proposition of our own foolishness, which we thereby confess; therefore no one who reasons, and consequently no one who participates, can be wise; in short, all men are fools.

TANS. I do not intend to infer that; for I will hold of highest wisdom him who could really say at one time the opposite of what he says at another--never was I less gay than now; or, never was I less sad than at present.

CIC. How? Do you not make two contrary qualities where there are two opposite affections? Why, I say, do you take as two virtues, and not as one vice and one virtue, the being less gay and the being less sad?

TANS. Because both the contraries in excess--that is, in so far as they exceed--are vices, because they pass the line; and the same, in so far as they diminish, come to be virtues, because they are contained within limits.

CIC. How? The being less merry and the being less sad are not one virtue and one vice, but are two virtues?

TANS. On the contrary, I say they are one and the same virtue; because the vice is there where the opposite is; the opposite is chiefly there where the extreme is; the greatest opposite is the nearest to the extreme; the least or nothing is in the middle, where the opposites meet, and are one and identical; as between the coldest and hottest and the hotter and colder, in the middle point is that which you may call hot and cold, or neither hot nor cold, without contradiction. In that way whoso is least content and least joyful is in the degree of indifference, and finds himself in the habitation of temperance, where the virtue and condition of a strong soul exist, which bends not to the south wind nor to the north. This, then, to return to the point, is how this enthusiastic hero, who explains himself in the present part, is different from the other baser ones--not as virtue from vice, but as a vice which exists in a subject more divine or divinely, from a vice which exists in a subject more savage or savagely; so that the difference is according to the different subjects and modes, and not according to the form of vice.

CIC. I can very well conceive, from what you have said, the condition of that heroic enthusiast, who says, "My hopes are ice and my desires are glowing," because he is not in the temperance of mediocrity, but, in the excess of contradictions, his soul is discordant, he shivers in his frozen hopes and burns in his glowing desires; in his eagerness he is clamorous, and he is mute from fear; his heart burns in its affection for others, and for compassion of himself he sheds tears from his eyes; dying in the laughter of others, he is alive in his own lamentations; and like him who no longer belongs to himself, he loves others and hates himself; because matter, as say the physicists, with that measure with which it loves the absent form, hates the present one. And so in the octave finishes the war which the soul has within itself; and when he says in the sistina, but if I be winged, others change to stone and that which follows; he shows his passion for the warfare which he wages with external contradictions. I remember having read in Jamblichus, where he treats of the Egyptian mysteries, this sentence: "Impius animam dissidentem habet: unde nec secum ipse convenire potest, neque cum aliis."

TANS. Now listen to another sonnet, as sequel to what has been said:

10. By what condition, nature, or fell chance,
In living death, dead life I live?
Love has me dead, alack! and such a death,
That death and life together I must lose.
Devoid of hope, I reach the gates of hell,
And laden with desire arrive at heaven:
Thus am I subject to eternal opposites,
And, banished both from heaven and from hell,
No pause nor rest my torments know,
Because between two running wheels I go,
Of which one here, the other there compels,

And like Ixion I pursue and flee;
For to the double discourse do I fit
The crosswise lesson of the spur and bit.

He shows how much he suffers from this dislocation and distraction in himself; while the affections, leaving the mean and middle way of temperance, tend towards the one and the other extreme, and so are wafted on high or towards the right, and are also transported downwards to the left.

CIC. How is it, that, not being really of one or the other extreme, it does not come to be in the conditions or terms of virtue?

TANS. It is then in a state of virtue when it keeps to the middle, declining from one to the other opposite; but when it leads towards the extremes, inclining to one or the other of those, it fails so entirely from being virtue, that it is a double vice, which consists in this, that the thing recedes from its nature, the perfection of which consists in unity, and there where the opposites meet, its composition and virtue exist. This, then, is how he is dead alive, or living dying; whence he says, "In a living death a dead life I live." He is not dead, because he lives in the object; not alive, because he is dead in himself; deprived of death, because he gives birth to thoughts; deprived of life, because he does not grow or feel in himself. He is now most dejected through meditating on the high intelligence, and the perceived feebleness of power; and most elated by the aspiration of heroic longing, which passes far beyond his limits, and is most exalted by the intellectual appetite; which has not for its fashion or aim to add number to number, is most dejected by the violence done to him by the sensual opposite which drags him down towards hell. So that, finding himself thus ascending and descending, he feels within his soul the greatest dissension that is possible to be felt, and he remains in a state of confusion through this rebellion of the senses, which urge him thither where reason restrains, and *vice versâ*. This same is thoroughly demonstrated in the following sentences, where the Reason, under the name of "Filenio" asks, and the enthusiast replies under the name of "Shepherd," who labours in the care of the flocks and herds of his thoughts, which he nourishes in the submission to and service of his nymph, which is the affection of that object to which he is captive.

    11. FILENIO. Shepherd!
SHEPHERD. What wilt thou?
F. What doest thou?
S. I suffer.
F. Wherefore?
S. Because neither life has me for his own, nor death.
F. Who's to blame
S. Love.
F. That rascal?
S. That rascal.
F. Where is he?
S. He holds me tight in my heart's core.
F. What does he?
S. Wounds me.
F. Who?
S. Me.
F. Thee?
S. Yes.
F. With what?
S. With the eyes, the gates of heaven and of hell.
F. Dost hope?
S. I hope.
F. For pity?
S. For pity.
F. From whom?
S. From him who racks me night and clay.
F. Has he any?
S. I know not.
F. Thou art a fool.
S. How if such folly be pleasing to my soul?
F. Does he promise?
S. No.
F. Does he deny?
S. Not at all.
F. Is he silent?
S. Yes, for so much purity (*omestà*) robs me of my boldness.
F. Thou ravest.

S, How so?
F. In vain efforts.
S. His scorn more than my torments do I fear.

Here he says that he craves for love, and he complains of it, yet not because he loves--seeing, that to no true lover can love be displeasing; but because he loves unhappily, whilst those beams which are the rays of those lights, and which themselves, according as they are perverse and antagonistic, or really kind and gracious, become the gates which lead towards heaven or towards hell. In this way he is kept in hope of future and uncertain mercy, but actually in a state of present and certain torment, and although he sees his folly quite clearly, nevertheless he does not care to correct himself in it, or even to feel displeased with it, but rather does he feel satisfied with it, as he shows when he says:

Never let me of Love complain,
For Love alone can ease my pain.

Here is shown another species of enthusiasm born from the light of reason, which excites fear and suppresses the aforesaid reason in order not to commit any action which might vex or irritate the thing loved. He says, then, that hope rests in the future, without anything being promised or denied; therefore, he is silent and asks nothing for fear of offending purity (*l'onestade*). He does not venture to explain himself and make a proposition, lest he be rejected with repugnance or accepted with reserve; for he thinks the evil that there might be in the one would be overbalanced by the good in the other. He shows himself, then, ready to suffer for ever his own torment, rather than to open the door to an opportunity through which the thing loved might be perturbed and saddened.

CIC. Herein he proves that his love is truly heroic; because he proposes to himself as the chief aim, not corporeal beauty, but rather the grace of the spirit, and the inclination of the affections in which, rather than in the beauty of the body, that love that has in it the divine, is eternal.

TANS. Thou knowes't that, as the Platonic ideas are divided into three species, of which one tends to the contemplative or speculative life, one to active morality, and the third to the idle and voluptuous, so are there three species of love, of which one raises itself from the contemplation of bodily form to the, consideration of the spiritual and divine; the other only continues in the delight of seeing and conversing; the third from seeing proceeds to precipitate into the concupiscence of touch. Of these three modes others are composed, according as the first may be coupled with the second or the third, or as all the three modes may combine together, of which one and all may be divided into others, according to the affections of the enthusiast, as these tend more towards the spiritual object, or more towards the corporeal, or equally towards the one and the other. Hence it comes, that of those who find themselves in this warfare, and are entangled in the meshes of love, some aim at enjoying, and they are incited to pluck the apple from the tree of corporeal beauty, without which acquisition, or at least the hope of it, they hold vain and worthy only of derision every amorous care; and in suchwise run all those who are of a barbarous nature, who neither do nor can seek to exalt themselves by loving worthy things, and aspiring to illustrious things, and higher still to things divine, by suitable studies and exercises, to which nothing can more richly and easily supply the wings than heroic love; others put before themselves the fruit of delight, which they take in the aspect of the beauty and grace of the spirit, which glitters and shines in the beauty of the body, and certain of these, although they love the body and greatly desire to be united to it, bewailing its absence and being afflicted by separation, at the same time fear, lest presuming in this they may be deprived of that affability, conversation, friendship, and sympathy which are most precious to them; because to attempt this there cannot be more guarantee of success than there is risk of forfeiting that favour, which appears before the eyes of thought as a thing so glorious and worthy.

CIC. It is a worthy thing, oh Tansillo! for its many virtues and perfections, and it behoves human genius to seek, accept, nourish, and preserve a love like that; but one should take great care not to, bow down or become enslaved to an object unworthy and base, lest we become sharers of the baseness and unworthiness of the same: appositely the Ferrarese poet says

Who sets his foot upon the amorous snare,
Lest he besmear his wings, let him beware.

TANS. To say the truth, that object, which beyond the beauty of the body has no other splendour, is not worthy of being loved otherwise than to make the race; and it seems to me the work of a pig or a horse to torment one's self about it, and as to myself, never was I more fascinated by such things than I am now fascinated by some statue or picture to which I am indifferent. It would then be a great dishonour to a generous soul, if, of a foul, vile, loose, and ignoble nature, although hid under an excellent symbol, it should be said: "I fear his scorn more than my torment."

Third Dialogue.

TANSILLO.
THERE are several varieties of enthusiasts, which may all be reduced to two kinds. While some only display blindness, stupidity, and irrational impetuosity, which tend towards savage madness, others by divine abstraction become in reality superior to ordinary men. And these again are of two kinds, for some having become the habitation of gods or divine spirits, speak and perform wonderful things, without themselves understanding the reason. Many such have been uncultured and ignorant persons, into whom, being void of spirit and sense of their own, as into an empty chamber, the divine spirit and sense intrude, as it would have less power to show itself in those who are full of their own reason and sense. This divine spirit often desires that the world should know for certain, that those do not speak from their own knowledge and experience, but speak and act through some superior intelligence; for such, the mass of men vouchsafe more admiration and faith, while others, being skilful in contemplation and possessing innately a clear intellectual spirit, have an internal stimulus and natural fervour, excited by the love of the divine, of justice, of truth, of glory, and by the fire of desire and the breath of intention, sharpen their senses, and in the sulphur of the cogitative faculty, these kindle the rational light, with which they see more than ordinarily; and they come in the end to speak and act, not as vessels and instruments, but as chief artificers and experts.

CIC. Of these two which dost thou esteem higher?

TANS. The first have more dignity, power, and efficacy within themselves, because they have the divinity; the second are themselves worthy, potential, and efficacious, and are divine. The first are worthy, as is the ass which carries the sacraments; the second are as a sacred thing. In the first is contemplated and seen in effect the divinity, and that is beheld, adored, and obeyed; in the second is contemplated and seen the excellency of humanity itself. But now to the question. These enthusiasms of which we speak, and which we see exemplified in these sentences, are not oblivion, but a memory;

they are not neglect of one's self, but love and desire of the beautiful and good, by means of which we are able to make ourselves perfect, by transforming and assimilating ourselves to it. It is not a precipitation, under the laws of a tyrannous fate, into the noose of animal affections, but a rational impetus, which follows the intellectual apprehension of the beautiful and the good, which knows whom it wishes to obey and to please, so that, by its nobility and light, it kindles and invests itself with qualities and conditions through which it appears illustrious and worthy. He (the enthusiast) becomes a god by intellectual contact with the divine object, and he has no thought for other than divine things, and shows himself insensible and impassive towards those things which are commonly felt, and about which others are mostly tormented; he fears nothing, and for love of the divine he despises other pleasures and gives no thought to this life. It is not, a fury of black bile which sends him drifting outside, of judgment, reason, and acts of prudence, and tossed by the discordant tempest, like those who, having violated certain laws of the divine Adrastia, are condemned to be scourged by the Furies, in order that they may be excited by a dissonance as corporeal through seditions, destructions, and plagues, as it is spiritual, through the forfeiture of harmony between the perceptive and enjoying powers; but ~t is a glow kindled by the intellectual sun in the soul, and a divine impetus which lends it wings, with which, drawing nearer and nearer to the intellectual sun, and ridding itself of the rust of human cares, it becomes a gold tried and pure, has the perception of divine and internal harmony, and its thoughts and acts accord with the symmetry of the law, innate in all things. Not, as drunk from the cups of Circe, does he go dashing and stumbling, now in this and then in that ditch, now against this or that rock, or like a shifting Proteus, changing now to this, now to the other aspect, never finding place, fashion, or ground to stay and settle in, but, without spoiling the harmony, conquers and overcomes the horrid monsters, and however much he may swerve, he easily returns to himself by means of those inward instincts that, like the nine Muses, dance and sing round the splendours of the universal Apollo, and under tangible images and material things, he comes to comprehend divine laws and counsels. It is true that sometimes, having love for his trusty escort, who is double, and because sometimes through occasional impediments he Ends himself defrauded of his strength, then, as one insane and furious, he squanders away the love of that which he cannot comprehend; whence, confused by the obscurity of the divinity, he sometimes abandons the work, and then again returns, to force himself with his will thither, where, he, cannot arrive with the intellect. It is true also that be commonly wanders, and transports himself, now into one, now into another form of the double, Eros; therefore, the principal lesson that Love gives to him is, that he contemplate the divine beauty in shadow, when he cannot do so in the mirror, and, like the suitors of Penelope, he entertain himself with the maids when he is not permitted to converse, with the mistress. Now, in conclusion, you can comprehend, from what has been said, what is this enthusiast whose picture is put forth, when it is said:

12. If towards the shining light the butterfly,
Winging his way knows not the burning flame,
And if the thirsty stag, unmindful of the dart,
Runs fainting to the brook,
Or unicorn, unto the chaste breast running,
Ignores the snare that is for him prepared,
I, in the light, the fount, the bosom of my love
Behold the flames, the arrows, and the chains.
If it be sweet in plaintiveness to droop,
Why does that lofty splendour dazzle me?
Wherefore the sacred arrow sweetly wound?
Why in this knot is my desire involved?
And why to me eternal irksomeness

Flames to my heart, darts to my breast and snares unto my soul?

Here he shows his love not to be like that of the butterfly, of the stag and of the unicorn, who would flee away if they had knowledge of the. fire, of the arrow, and of the snares, and who have no other sense than that of pleasure; but he is moved by a most sensible and only too evident passion, which forces him to love that fire more than any coolness; more that wound than any wholeness; more those fetters than any liberty. For this evil is not absolutely evil, but, through comparison with good (according to opinion), it is deceptive, like the sauce that old Saturn gets when he devours his own sons; for this evil absolutely in the eye of the Eternal, is comprehended either for good, or for guide which conduces to it, since this fire is the ardent desire of divine things, this arrow is the impression of the ray of the beauty of supernal light, these snares are the species of truth which unite our mind to the, primal verity, and the species of good which unite and join to the primal and highest good. To that meaning I approached when I said:

13. With such a fire and such a noble noose,
Beauty enkindles me, and pureness binds,
So that in flames and servitude I take delight,
Liberty takes flight and dreads the ice.
Such is the heat, that though I burn yet am I not destroyed,
    The tie is such, the world with me gives praise.
    Fear cannot freeze, nor pain unshackle me;
    For soothing is the ardour, sweet the smart.
    So high the light that burns me I discern,
    And of so rich a thread the noose contrived
    That, thought being born, the longing dies.
    And since, within my heart shines such pure flames,
    And so supreme a tie compels my will,
    Let, my shade serve, and let ray ashes burn.

All the loves, if they be heroic and not purely animal, or what is called natural, and slaves to generation, as instruments of nature in a certain way, have for object the divinity, tend towards divine beauty, which first is communicated to souls and shines in them, and from them, or rather through them, it is communicated to bodies; whence it is that well-ordered affection loves the body or corporeal beauty, insomuch as it is an indication of beauty of spirit. Thus that which causes the attraction of love to the body is a certain spirituality which we see in it, and which is called beauty, and which does not consist in major or minor dimensions, nor in determined colours or forms, but in harmony and consonance of members and colours. This shows an affinity between the spirit and the most acute and penetrative senses; whence it follows that such become more easily and intensely enamoured, and also more easily and intensely disgusted, which might be through a change of the deformed spirit, which in some gesture and expressed intention reveals itself in such wise that this deformity extends from the soul to the body, and makes it appear no longer beautiful as before. The beauty, then, of the body has power to kindle, but not to bind, and the lover, unless aided by the graces of the spirit, such as purity, gratitude, courtesy, circumspection, is unable to escape. Therefore, said I, beautiful is that fire which burns me, and noble that tie which binds.

CIC. I do not believe it is always like that, Tansillo; because, sometimes, notwithstanding that we discover the spirit to be vicious, we remain heated and entangled; so that, although reason perceives the evil and unworthiness of such a love, it yet has not power to alienate the disordered appetite. In this disposition, I believe, was the Nola-no when he said:

Woe's me! my fury forces me
To union with the bad within,
And makes it seem a love supreme and good.
Wearied, my soul cares nought
That I opposing counsels entertain,
And with the savage, tyrant
Nourished with want,
And made to put myself in exile,
More than with liberty contented am.
I spread my sails to the wind,
To draw me forth from this detested bliss,
And I reclaim me from the cloying hurt.

TANS. This occurs when spirits are vicious and tinged as with the same hue; since, through conformity, love is excited, enkindled, and confirmed. Thus the vicious easily concur in acts of the same vice; and I will not refrain from repeating that which I know by experience, for although I may have discovered in a soul vices very much abominated by me--as, for instance, filthy avarice, base greediness for money, ingratitude for favours and courtesies received, or a love of quite vile persons, of which this last most displeases, because it takes away the hope from the lover, that by becoming or making himself more worthy he may become more acceptable--in spite of all this, it is trite that I did burn for corporeal beauty. But how? I loved against my will; for, were it not so, I should have been more, saddened than cheered by troubles and misfortunes.

CIC. It is a very proper and nice distinction that is made between loving and liking.

TANS. Truly; because we like many--that is, we desire that they be wise and just; but we love them not because they are unjust and ignorant; many we love because they are beautiful, but we do not like them, because they do not deserve it; and amongst other things of which the lover deems the loved one undeserving, the first is, being loved; and yet, although he cannot abstain from loving, nevertheless he regrets it, and shows his regret like him who said, "Woe is me! who am compelled by passion to coalesce with evil." In the opposite mood was he, either through some corporeal object in similitude or through a divine subject in reality, when he said:

15. Although to many pains thou dost subject me,
Yet do I thank thee, love, and owe thee much,
That thou my breast dost cleave with noble wound,
And then dost take my heart and master it.
Thus true it is, that I, on earth, adore
A living object, image most beautiful of God.
Let him who will think that my fate is bad
That kills in hope and quickens in desire.
My pasture is the high emprise,
And though the end desired be not attained,
And though my soul in many thoughts is spent,
Enough that she enkindle noble fire,
Enough that she has lifted me on high,
And from the ignoble crowd has severed me.

Here his love is entirely heroic and divine, and as such, I wish it to be understood, although he says that through it he is subject to many pangs, every lover who is separated from the thing loved (to which being joined by affection he would also wish to be actually), being in anguish and pain, he torments himself, not forsooth because he loves, since he feels his love is engaged most worthily and most nobly, but because he feels deprived of that fruition which he would obtain if he arrived at that end to which he tends. He suffers, not from the desire which animates him, but from the difficulty in the cultivation of it which so tortures him. Others esteem him unhappy through this appearance of an evil destiny, as being condemned to these pangs, for he will never cease from acknowledging the obligation he is under to love, nor cease from rendering thanks to him because he has presented before the eyes of his mind such an intelligible conception through which, in this earthly life, shut in this prison of the flesh, wrapped in these nerves and supported by these bones, it is permitted to him to contemplate the divinity in a more suitable manner than if other conceptions and similitudes than these had offered themselves.

CIC. The divine and living object, then, of which he speaks, is the highest intelligible conception that he has been able to form to himself of the divinity, and is not some corporeal beauty which might overshadow his thought and appear superficially to the senses.

TANS. Even so; because no tangible thing nor conception of such can raise itself to so much dignity.

CIC. Why, then, does be mention that conception as the object, if, as appears to me, the true object is the divinity itself?

TANS. The divinity is the final object, the ultimate and most perfect, but not in this state, where we cannot see God except as in a, shadow or a mirror, and therefore He cannot be the object except in some similitude, but not in such as may be extracted or acquired from corporeal beauty and excellence, by virtue of the senses, but such as may be formed in the mind, by virtue of the intellect. In which state, finding himself, he comes to lose the love and affection for every other thing senseful as well as intellectual, because this, conjoined to that light, itself also becomes light, and in consequence becomes a god: because it contracts the divinity into itself, it being in God through the intention with which it penetrates into the divinity so far as it can, and God being in it, so that after penetrating it comes to conceive, and so far as it can, receive and comprehend. the divinity in its conception. Now in such conceptions and similitudes the human intellect of this lower world nourishes itself, till such time as it, will be lawful to behold with purer eye the beauty of the divinity. As happens to him, who, absorbed in the contemplation of some elaborate architectural work, goes on examining one thing after another in it, enchanted and feeding in a wonder of delight; but if it should happen that he sees the lord of all those pictures, who is of a beauty incomparably greater, leaving all care and thought of them, he is turned intently to the examination of him. Here, then, is the difference between that state where we see divine beauty in intelligible conceptions apart from the effects, labours, works, shadows, and similitudes of it, and that other state in which it is lawful to behold it in real presence. He says: "My pasture is the high emprise," because as the Pythagoreans remark, "The soul moves and turns round God, as the body round the soul."

CIC. Then the body is not the habitation of the soul?

TANS. No; because the soul is not in the body locally, but as intrinsic form and extrinsic framer, as that which forms the limbs indicates the internal and external composition. The body, then, is in the soul, the soul in the mind, the mind either is God or is in God, as Plotinus said. As in its essence it, is in God who is its life, similarly through the intellectual operation, and the will consequent upon such operation, it agrees with its bright and beatific object. Fitly, therefore, this rapture of heroic enthusiasm feeds on such "high emprise." For the object is infinite, and in action most simple, and our intellectual power cannot apprehend the infinite except in speech or in a certain manner of speech, so to say in a certain potential or relative inference, as one who proposes to himself the infinite, so that he may constitute for himself a finality where no finality is.

CIC. Fitly so, because the ultimate ought not to have an end seeing that it is ultimate. For it is infinite in intention, in perfection, in essence, and in any other manner whatsoever of being final.

TANS. Thou sayest truly. Now in this life, that food is such that excites more than it can appease, as that divine poet shows when he says: "My soul is wearied, longing for the living God," and in another place; "Attenuati sunt oculi mei suspicientes in excelsa." Therefore he says, "And though the end desired be not attained, And that my soul in many thoughts is spent, Enough that she enkindle noble fire:" meaning to say that the soul comforts itself, and receives all the glory which it is able in that state to receive, and that it is a participator in that ultimate enthusiasm of man, in so far as he is a man in this present condition, as we see him.

CIC. It appears to me that the Peripatetics, as explained by Averroes, mean this, when they say that the highest felicity of man consists in perfection through the speculative sciences.

TANS. It is true, and they say well; because we, in this state, cannot desire nor obtain greater perfection than that in which we are, when our intellect, by means of some noble and intelligible conception, unites itself either to the substance of things hoped for, as those say, or to the divine mind, as it is the fashion to say of the Platonists. For the present, I will leave reasoning about the soul, or man in another state or mode of being than be can find himself or believe himself to be in.

CIC. But what perfection or satisfaction can man find in that knowledge which is not perfect?

TANS. It will never be perfect, so far as understanding the highest object is concerned; but in so far as our intellect can understand it. Let it suffice that in this and other states there be present to him the divine beauty so far as the horizon of his vision extends.

CIC. But all men cannot arrive at that, which one or two may reach.

TANS. Let it suffice that all "run well," and that each does his utmost, for the heroic nature is content and shows its dignity rather in falling, or in failing worthily in the high undertaking, in which it shows the dignity of its spirit, than in succeeding to perfection in lower and less noble things.

CIC. Truly a dignified and heroic death is better than a mean, low triumph.

TANS. On that theme I made this sonnet:
16. Since I have spread my wings to my desire,
The more I feel the air beneath my feet,

So much the more towards the wind I bend
My swiftest pinions,
And spurn the world and up towards heaven I go.
Not the sad fate of Daedalus's son
Does warn me to turn downwards,
But ever higher will I rise.
Well do I see, I shall fall dead to earth;
But what life is there can compare with this my death?
Out on the air my heart's voice do I hear:
"Whither dost thou carry me, thou fearless one?
Turn back. Such over-boldness rarely grief escapes."
Fear not the utmost ruin then," I said,
Cleave confident the clouds and die content,
That heaven has destined thee to such illustrious death."

CIC. I understand when you say: "Enough that thou hast lifted me on high;" but not: "And from the ignoble crowd hast severed me;" unless it means his having come out from the Platonic groove on account of the stupid and low condition of the crowd; for those, that find profit in this contemplation cannot be numerous.

TANS. Thou understandest well; but thou mayst also understand, by the "ignoble crowd," the body, and sensual cognition, from which he must arise and free himself who would unite with a nature of a contrary kind.

CIC. The Platonists say there are two kinds of knots which link the soul to the body. One is a certain vivifying action which from the soul descends into the body, like a ray; the other is a certain vital quality, which is produced from that action in the body. Now this active and most noble number, which is the soul, in what way do you understand that it may be severed from the ignoble number, which is the body?

TANS. Certainly it was not understood according to any of these modes, but according to that mode whereby, those powers which are not comprehended and imprisoned in the womb of matter, sometimes as if inebriated and stupefied, find that they also are occupied in the formation of matter and in the vivification of the body; then, as if awakened and brought to themselves, recognizing its principle and genius, they turn towards superior things and force themselves on the intelligible world as to their native abode, and from thence, through their conversion to inferior things, they are thrust into the fate and conditions of generation. These two impulses are symbolized in the two kinds of metamorphosis expressed in the following:

17. That god who shakes the sounding thunder,
Asteria as a furtive eagle saw;
Mnemosyne as shepherd; Danae gold;
Alcmene as a fish: Antiope a goat;
Cadmus and his sister a white bull;
Leda as swan, and Dolida as dragon;
And through the lofty object I become,
From subject viler still, a god.
A horse was Saturn;
And in a calf and dolphin Neptune dwelt;
Ibis and shepherd Mercury became;
Bacchus a grape; Apollo was a crow;
And I by help of love,
From an inferior thing, do change we to a god.

In Nature is one revolution and one circle, by means of which, for the perfection and help of others, superior things lower themselves to things inferior, and, by their own excellence and felicity, inferior things raise themselves to superior ones. Therefore the Pythagoreans and Platonists say it is given to the soul that at certain times, not only by spontaneous will, which turns it to-wards, tae comprehension of Nature, but also by the, necessity of an internal law, written and registered by the destined decree, they seek their own justly determined fate; and they also say that souls, not so much by determination. of their own will as through a certain order, by which they become inclined towards matter, decline as rebels from divinity; wherefore, not by free intention, but by a certain occult consequence, they fall. And this is the inclination that they have to generation, as towards a minor good. Minor, I say, in so far as it appertains to that particular nature; not in so far as it appertains to the universal nature, where nothing happens without the highest aim, and which disposes of all things according to justice. In which generation finding themselves once more through the changes which permutably succeed, they return again to the superior forms.

CIC. So that they mean, that souls are impelled by the necessity of fate, and have no proper counsel which guides them at all.

TANS. Necessity, fate, nature, counsel, will, those things, justly and rightfully ordained, all agree in one. Besides which, as Plotinus relates, some believe that certain souls can escape from their own evil, if knowing the danger, they seek refuge in the mind before the corporeal habit is confirmed; because the mind raises to things sublime, as the imagination lowers to inferior things. The mind always understands one, as the imagination is one in movement and in diversity; the mind always understands one, as the imagination is always inventing for itself various images. In the midst is the rational faculty, which is a mixture of all, like that in which the one agrees with the many, sameness with variety, movement with fixedness, the inferior with the superior. Now these transmutations and con versions are symbolized in the wheel of metamorphosis, where man sits on the upper part, a beast lies at the bottom, a half-man, half-beast descends from the left, and a half-beast, half-man ascends from the right. This transmutation is shown where Jove, according to the diversity of the affections and the behaviour of those towards inferior things, invests himself with divers figures, entering into the form of beasts; and so also the other gods transmigrate into base and alien forms. And, on the contrary, through the knowledge of their own nobility, they re-take their own divine form; as the passionate hero, raising himself through conceived kinds of divine beauty and goodness, with the wings of the intellect and rational will, rises to the divinity, leaving the form of the lower subject. And therefore he said, "I become from subject viler still, a god. From in inferior thing do change me to a god."

FOURTH DIALOGUE

TANSILLO
THUS is described the discourse of heroic love, in all which tends to its own object, which is the highest good; and heroic intellect, which devotes itself to the study of its own object, which is the primal verity, or absolute truth. Now the first discourse holds the sum of this and the intention, the order of which is described in five others following:

18. To the woods, the mastiffs and the greyhounds young Actæon leads,
When destiny directs him into the doubtful and neglected
Upon the track of savage beasts in forests wild.
And here, between the waters, he sees a bust and face more beautiful than e'er was seen
By mortal or divine, of scarlet, alabaster, and fine gold;
He sees: and the great hunter straight becomes that which he hunts.
The stag, that towards still thicker shades now goes with lighter steps,
His own great dogs swiftly devour.
So I extend my thoughts to higher prey, and these
Now turning on me give me death with cruel savage bite.

Actæon signifies the intellect, intent on the pursuit of divine wisdom and the comprehension of divine beauty. He lets loose the mastiffs and the greyhounds, of whom the latter are more swift and the, former more strong, because the operation of the intellect precedes that of the will; but this is more. vigorous and effectual than that; seeing that, to the human intellect, divine goodness and beauty are more loveable than comprehensible, and love it is that moves and urges the intellect, and precedes it as a lantern. The woods, uncultivated and solitary places, visited and penetrated by few, and where there are few traces of men. The, youth of little skill and practice, as of one of short life and of wavering enthusiasm. In the doubtful road of uncertain and distorted reason--a disposition assigned to the character of Pythagoras--where you see the most thorny, uncultivated, and deserted to be the right and difficult path, where he lets loose the greyhounds and the mastiffs upon the track of savage beasts, that is, the intelligible kinds of ideal conceptions, which are occult, followed by few, visited but rarely, and which do not disclose themselves to all those who seek them. Here, amongst the waters,--that is, in the mirror of similitude, in those works where shines the brightness of divine goodness and splendour, which works are symbolized by the waters superior and inferior, which are above and below the firmament, he sees the most beautiful bust and face--that is, external power and operation, which it is possible to see, by the habit and act of contemplation and the application of mortal or divine mind, of man or any god.

CIC. I do not believe that he makes a comparison, nor puts as the same kind the divine and the human mode of comprehending, which are. very diverse, but as to the subject they are the same.

TANS. So it is. He says "of red and alabaster and gold," because that which in bodily beauty is red, white, and fair, in divinity signifies the scarlet of divine vigorous power, the gold of divine wisdom, the alabaster of divine beauty, through the contemplation of which the Pythagoreans, Chaldeans, Platonists, and others, strive in the best way that they can to elevate themselves. "The great hunter saw," he understood as much as was possible, and became the hunted. He went out for prey, and this hunter became himself the prey, by the operation of the intellect converting the things learned into itself.

CIC. I understand. He forms intelligible conceptions in his own way and proportions them to his capacity, so that they are received according to the manner of the recipient.

TANS. And does he hunt through the operation of the will, by the act of which he converts himself into the object?

CIC. As I understand: because love transforms and converts into the thing loved.

TANS. Well dost thou know that the intellect learns things intelligibly--*i.e.*, in its own way, and the will pursues things naturally, that is, according to the reason that is in themselves. So Actæon with those thoughts--those dogs--which hunted outside themselves for goodness, wisdom, and beauty, thus came into the presence of the same, and ravished out of himself by so much splendour, he became the prey, saw himself converted into that for which he was seeking, and perceived, that of his dogs or thoughts, he himself came to be the longed for prey; for having absorbed the divinity into himself it was not necessary to search outside himself for it.

CIC. For this reason it is said "the kingdom of Heaven is in us;" divinity dwells within through the reformed intellect and will.

TANS. It is so. See then, Actæon hunted by his own dogs--pursued by his own thoughts--runs and directs these novel paces, invigorated so as to proceed divinely and "more easily," that is, with greater facility and with refreshed vigour "towards the denser places," to the deserts and the region of thing s incomprehensible. From being such as he first was, a common ordinary man, he becomes rare and heroic, his habits and ideas are strange, and he leads an unusual life. Here his great dogs "give him death," and thus ends his life according to the mad, sensual, blind, and fantastic world, and he begins to live intellectually; he lives the life of the gods, fed on ambrosia and drunk with nectar.

Next we see under the form of another Similitude the manner in which he arms himself to obtain the object. He says:

19. My solitary bird! away unto that region
Which overshadows and which occupies my thought,
Go swiftly, and there nestle; there every
Need of thine be strengthened,
There all thy industry and art be spent!
There be thou born again, and there on high,
Gather and train up thy wandering fledglings
Since adverse fate has drawn away the bars
With which she ever sought to block thy way.
Go! I desire for thee a nobler dwelling-place,
And thou shalt have for guide a god,
Who is called blind by him who nothing sees.
Go! and ever be by thee revered,
Each deity of that wide sphere,
And come not back to me till thou art mine.

The progress symbolized above by the hunter who excites his dogs, is here illustrated by a winged heart, which is sent out of the cage, in which it lived idle and quiet, to make its nest on high and bring up its fledglings, its thoughts, the time being come in which those impediments are removed, which were caused, externally, in a thousand different ways, and internally by natural feebleness. He dismisses his heart then to make more magnificent surroundings, urging him to the highest propositions and intentions, now that those powers of the soul are more fully fledged, which Plato signifies by the two wings, and he commits him to the guidance of that god, who, by the unseeing crowd, is considered insane and blind, that is Love, who, by the mercy and favour of heaven, has power to transform him into that nature towards which he aspires, or into that state from which, a pilgrim, he is banished. Whence he says, "Come not back to me till thou art mine," and not unworthily may I say with that other--

Thou has left me, oh, my heart,
And thou, light of my eyes, art no more with me.

Here he describes the death of the soul, which by the Kabbalists is called the death by kisses, symbolized in the Song of Solomon, where the friend says:

Let him kiss me with the kisses of his mouth,
For, when he wounds me,
I suffer with a cruel love.

By others it is called sleep; the Psalmist says
It shall be, that give sleep unto mine eyes,
And mine eyelids shall slumber,
And I shall have in him peaceful repose.

The soul then is said to be faint, because it is dead in itself, and alive in the object:

20. Give heed, enthusiasts, unto the heart!
For mine condemns me to a life apart,
Bound by unmerciful and cruel ties,
He dwells with joy, there where he faints and dies.
At every hour I call him back by thoughts:
A rebel he, like gerfalcon insane,
He feels no more the hand that did restrain,
And is I one forth not to return again.
Thou beauteous beast that dost in punishment
Knit up the soul, spirit and heart content'st

With pricks, with lightnings, and with chains!
From looks, from accents, and from usages,
Which faint and burn and keep thee bound,
Where shall he that heals, that cools, and loosens thee be found?

Here the soul, sorrowful, not from real discontent, but on account of pains which she suffers, directs the discourse to those who are affected by passions similar to her own: as if she had not of her own free will and of her own desire dismissed her heart, which goes running whither it cannot arrive, stretches out to that which it cannot reach, and tries to enfold that which it cannot comprehend, and with this, because he vainly separates from her, ever more and more goes on aspiring towards the infinite.

CIC. Whence comes it, oh Tansillo, that the soul in such progression delights in its own torments? Whence comes that spur which urges it ever beyond that which it possesses?

TANS. From this, which I will tell thee now. The intellect being developed to the comprehension of a certain definite and specific form, and the will to a love commensurate with such comprehension; the intellect does not stop there, bat by its own light it is prompted to think of this: that it contains within itself the germ of everything intelligible and desirable, until it comes to comprehend with the intellect the depth of the fountain of ideas, the ocean of every truth and goodness. So that it happens, that whatever conception is presented to the mind, and becomes understood by it, from that which is so presented and comprehended it judges, that above it, is other greater and greater, and finds itself ever in a certain way discoursing and moving with it. Because it sees that all which it possesses is only a limited thing, and therefore cannot be sufficient of itself, nor good of itself, nor beautiful of itself; because it is not the universal nor the absolute entity; but contracted into being this nature, this species, this form, represented to the intellect and present to the soul. Then from the beautiful that is understood, and consequently limited, and therefore beautiful through participation, it progresses towards that which is really beautiful, which has no margin, nor any boundaries.

CIC. This progression appears to me useless.

TANS. Not so. For it is not natural nor suitable that the infinite be restricted, nor give itself definitely, for it would not then be infinite. To be infinite, it must be infinitely pursued with that form of pursuit which is not incited physically, but metaphysically, and is not from imperfect to perfect, but goes circulating through the grades of perfection to arrive at that infinite centre which is not form, and is not formed.

CIC. I should like to know how, by circumambulating, one is to arrive at the centre?

TANS. I cannot know that.

CIC. Why do you say it?

TANS. I can say it, and leave it to you to consider.

CIC. If you do not mean that he who pursues the infinite is like him who talks about the circumference when he is seeking for the centre, I do not know what you mean.

TANS. Quite the contrary.

CIC. Now if you will not explain yourself, I cannot understand you; but tell me, prythee, what he means by saying the heart is bound by cruel, spiteful bonds.

TANS. He speaks in similitude or metaphor; as you would say, cruel was one who did not allow a full enjoyment, and who lives more in the desire than in possession, and who, partially possessing, is not content, but desires, faints, and dies.

CIC. What are those thoughts that call him back from the noble enterprise?

TAMS. The sensual and natural affections, which regard the government of the body.

CIC. What have they to do with it, that in no way can either help or favour it?

TANS. They have not to do with it, but with the, soul, which, being so absorbed in one work or study, becomes remiss and careless in others.

CIC. Why does he call him insane?

TANS. Because he surpasses in knowledge.

CIC. It is usual to call insane those, who know nothing.

TANS. On the contrary. Those are called insane who know not in the ordinary way, or who rise above the ordinary from having more intellect.

CIC. I perceive that thou sayest truly. Now tell me what are the pricks, the lightnings, and the chains?

TANS. Pricks are those experiences that stimulate and awaken the affection, to make it on the alert; lightnings are the rays of the present beauty, which enlighten those who watch and wait for them; chains are those effects and circumstances which keep fixed the eyes of attention and unite together the object and the powers.

CIC. What are the looks, the accents, and the customs?

TANS. Looks are the means by which the object is made present to us; accents are the means through which we are inspired and informed; customs are the circumstances which are most pleasant and agreeable to us. So that the heart that gently suffers, patiently burns and constantly perseveres in the work, fears that its hurt will heal, its fire be extinguished, and its bands be loosened.

CIC. Now relate that which follows.

TANS.:

21. Lofty, profound, and stirring thoughts of mine,
Ye long to sever the maternal ties
Of the afflicted soul, and like to proud
And able bowmen, draw at the mark,
"Which is the germ of all your high conceits.
In those steep paths where cruel beasts may be,
Let not heaven leave ye!
Remember to return, and summon back
The heart that tarries with the wild wood nymph;
Arm ye with love,
Warn with the flame of domesticity,
And with strong repression guard thy sight,
That strangers keep thee not companioned with my heart;
At least bring news of that,
Which unto him is such delight and joy.

Here he describes the natural solicitude of the attentive soul on the subject, of its inclination towards generation, which it has contracted with matter. She dispatches the armed thoughts, which, solicited and urged by disagreement with the inferior nature, are sent to recall the heart. The soul instructs them how they should conduct themselves, so that, being allured and attracted by the object, they do not become induced to remain, they also, captive and companions of the heart. She says, then, they are to arm themselves with love, with that love that is fired by the domestic flame; that is, the friend of generation, to whom they are bound, and in whose jurisdiction, ministry, and warfare they find themselves. Anon she orders them to repress their eyesight and to close their eyes, so that they may not behold other beauty or goodness than that which is present, friend and mother; and concludes at last with this, that if no other reason will cause them to return, they should at least do so, to give account of the discourse and of the state of the heart.

CIC. Before you proceed further, I would understand from you what is that which the soul means when she tells the thoughts to repress the sight vigorously.

TANS. I will tell thee. All love proceeds from seeing: intelligent love, from seeing intelligently; sensuous love, from seeing sensuously. Now this seeing has two meanings: either it means the visual power, that is the sight, which is the intellect, or truly the sense; or it means the act of that power, that is, that application which the eye or the intellect makes to the material or intellectual object. When the thoughts are counselled to repress the sight, it is not the first, but the second, mode that is meant, because that is the father of the subsequent affection of the sensuous or intellectual desire.

CIC. This is what I wished to hear from you. Now, if the act of the visual power is the cause of the evil or good which proceed from seeing, whence comes it that in things divine we have more love, than knowledge?

TANS. We desire to see, because in some way we perceive the value of seeing. We are aware that, through the act of seeing, beautiful things offer themselves to us; and therefore we desire beautiful things.

CIC. We desire the beautiful and the good; but seeing is not beautiful nor good, rather is it the touchstone or light by which we see, not only the beautiful. and good, but also the evil and bad. Therefore it seems to me that seeing may be equally beautiful or good, as the thing seen may be white or black. If, then, the sight, which is an act, is not beautiful nor good, how can it fall into desire?

TANS. If not for itself, yet certainly for some other reason, it is desired, seeing that there can be no apprehension of that other without it.

CIC. What wilt thou say, if that other is not within the knowledge of the, senses nor of the intellect? How, I say, can that be desired which is not seen, if there is no knowledge whatever of it--if towards it neither the intellect nor the sense has exercised any act whatever; but, on the contrary, it is even dubious whether it be intellectual or sensuous, whether a thing corporeal or incorporeal, whether it be one or two or more, or of one fashion or of another?

TANS. I answer, that in the sense and the intellect there is one desire and one impulse to the sensuous in general; because the intellect will hear the whole truth, so that it may learn all that is beautiful or good intelligently; the power of the senses will inform itself of all that is sensuous, so that it may know all that is good and beautiful in the world of the senses. Hence it follows that not less do we desire to see things unknown and unseen than those known and seen. And from this it does not follow that the desire does not proceed from cognition, and that we desire something that is not known; but I say that it is certain and sure that we do not desire unknown things. Because, if they be occult as to particulars, they are not occult as to generals; as in the entire visual power is found the whole of the visible appositely, and in the intellect all the intelligible. Therefore, as the inclination to the act lies in its appropriateness, the result is that both these powers incline towards the universal action, as to a thing naturally comprehended as good. The soul, then, did not speak to the deaf or the blind when she counselled her thoughts to repress the sight, which, although it may not be the immediate cause of the will, is yet the primal and principal cause.

CIC. What do you mean by this last saying?

TANS. I mean that it is not the figure or the conception, sensibly or intelligently represented, which of itself moves us; because while one stands beholding the figure manifested to the eyes, he does not yet arrive at loving; but from that instant that the soul conceives within itself that figure, not visible, but thinkable; no longer dividual, but individual; no longer classed among things in general, but among things good and beautiful; then immediately love is born. Now this is the seeing, from which the soul desires to divert the eyes of her thoughts. Here the sight usually moves the affection to a greater love than the love of that which is seen; for, as I have just said, it always considers, through the universal knowledge that it holds of the beautiful and the good, that, besides the degrees of known conceptions of goodness and beauty, there are others and yet others *ad infinitum*.

CIC. How is it that after we become informed of that conception of the beautiful which is begotten in the soul, we yet desire to satisfy the exterior vision?

TANS. From this, that the soul would ever love that which it loves, and ever see that which it sees. Therefore she wills that, the conception which has been produced in her through seeing, should not become weakened, enervated and lost; but would ever see more and more, and that which becomes obscure in the interior affection, should be frequently brightened by the exterior aspect, which as it is the principle of being, must also be the principle of conservation. This results proportionately in the act of understanding and of considering, for as the sight has reference to visible things, so has the, intellect to intelligible things. I believe now that you understand to what end and in what manner the soul tends, when she says "repress the sight."

CIC. I understand very well. Now continue to unfold what happens to these thoughts.

TANS. Now follows the disagreement between the mother and the aforesaid children, who having, contrary to her orders, opened their eyes, and, having fixed them on the splendour of the object, they remained in company with the heart.

22. Cruel sons are ye to me, me whom ye left
Still farther to exasperate my pain;
And ever without cease ye weary me,
Taking away from me my every hope!
Why should the sense remain? oh, grasping heavens!

Wherefore these broken ruined powers, if not
To make me subject and exemplar
Of such heavy martyrdom, such lengthened pain?
Leave, dear sons, my winged fire enchained,
And let me, some of you once more behold,
Come back to me from those retaining claws!
Oh, weariness! not one returns
To bring a late refreshment to my pains.

Behold me, miserable one, deprived of heart, abandoned of thoughts, left by hope, I, who had fixed my all in them. Nothing is left to me but the sense of my poverty, my unhappiness and misery; why does not this too leave me? Why does not death succour me, now that I am deprived of life? To what use do I possess these natural powers if I be deprived of the use of them? How can I alone nourish myself with intelligible conceptions as with intellectual bread, if the substance of this bread be composed of this contingency. How can I linger in the intimacy of these friendly and dear members which I have woven round me, adjusting them with the symmetry of the elementary conditions, if my thoughts and all my affections abandon me, intent upon the care of the bread that is immaterial and divine? Up, up; oh, my flying thoughts; up, oh my rebel heart; let live the sense of things that are felt, and the understanding of things intelligible, come to the succour of the body with matter and corporeal subject, and let the understanding delight in its own objects to the end that this composition of the body may be realized, that this machine dissolve not, in which, by means of the spirit, the soul is united to the body. Why, unhappy as I am (more through domestic circumstances than through external violence), am I doomed to see this horrible divorce between my parts and members? Why does the intellect trouble itself to give laws to the sense and yet deprive it of its food? and this, on the other hand, resists; desiring to live according to its own decrees, and not according to the decree of others; for these and not those are able to maintain and bless it, therefore it ought to attend to its own comfort and life, and not to that of others. There is no harmony and concord where there is only one, where one individual absorbs the whole being, but where there is order and analogy in things diverse; where each thing serves its own nature. Therefore lot the sense feed according to the law of things that can be felt, the flesh be obedient to the? law of the spirit, the reason to its own law. Let them not be confounded nor mixed. Enough that one neither mar nor prejudice the law of the other, since it is not just that the sense outrage the law of reason. And verily it is a shameful thing that one, should tyrannize over the other, particularly where the intellect is a pilgrim and strange, and the sense is more domesticated and at home. I am forced by you, my thoughts, to remain at home in charge of the house, while others may wander wherever they will. This is a law of Nature, and therefore a law of the author and originator of Nature. Sin on then, now that all of you, seduced by the charm of the intellect, leave the other part of me to the peril of death. How have you gotten this melancholy and perverse humour, which breaks the certain and natural laws of the true life, and which is in your own hands, for one, uncertain, and which has no existence except in shadow, beyond the limits of fantastic thought? Seems it to you a natural thing that they should live divinely and not as animals and humanly, they being not gods, but men and animals? It is a law of fate and Nature that everything should adapt itself to the condition of its own being, wherefore then, while you follow after the niggard nectar of the gods, do you lose that which is present and is your own, and trouble yourself about the vain hopes of others? Ought not Nature to refuse to give you the other good, if that which she at present offers to you,. you stupidly despise?

Heaven the second gift denies,
To him who does the first despise.

With these and similar reasons the soul, taking part with the weakest, seeks to recall the thoughts to the care of the body. And these, although late, come and show themselves, but not in that form in which they departed, but only to declare their rebellion, and force her to follow. And the sorrowing one thus laments:

23. Ah, dogs of Actæon, ah, proud ingrates!
Whom to the abode of my divinity I sent;
Without hope do ye return to me;

And, coming to the mother's side, ye bring
Back unto me a too unhappy boon;
Ye mangle me, and will that I live not.
Leave me, life, that I may mount up to my sun,
A double streamlet, mad, without my fount!
When shall this ponderous mass of me dissolve?
When shall it be, that, taking myself hence,
And swiftly rising to the heights above,
Together with my heart I may abide,
And with my thoughts I may be deified?

The Platonists say that the soul, as to its superior part, always consists in the intellect, in which it has more of understanding than of soul, seeing that it is called soul only in so far as it vivifies the body and sustains it. So here, the same essence which nourishes and maintains the thoughts on high, together with the exalted heart, is induced by the inferior part to afflict itself, and recall them as rebels.

CIC. So that they are not two contrary existences, but one, subject to two contradictory terms?

TANS. So it is, precisely. As the ray of the sun which touches the earth, and is joined to obscure and to inferior things, which it brightens, vivifies, and kindles, and is then joined to the element of fire--that is, to the star, whence it proceeds, and has its beginning, and is diffused, and in which it has its own and original subsistence--so the soul, which is in the horizon of Nature, is corporeal and incorporeal, and contains that with which it rises to superior things and declines to things inferior. And this, you may perceive, does not happen by reason and order of local motion, but solely through the impulse of one and of another power or faculty. As when the sense rises to the imagination, the imagination to the reason, the reason to the intellect, the intellect to the mind, then the whole soul is converted into God, and inhabits the intelligible world; whence, on the other hand, she descends in an inverse manner to the world of feeling, through the intellect, reason, imagination, sense, vegetation.

CIC. It is true that I have heard that the soul, in order to put itself in the ultimate degree of divine things, descends into the mortal body, and from this goes up again to the divine degrees, which are three degrees of intelligence. For there are others in which the intellectual surpasses the animal, which are said to be the celestial intelligences; and others in which the animal surpasses the intellectual, which are the human intelligences; others there are, of which those things are equal, as those of demons or heroes.

TANS. The mind then cannot desire except that which is near, close, known, and familiar. The pig cannot desire to be a man, nor wish for those things that are suitable to the human appetite. He likes better to turn about in mud than in a bed of linen, he would prefer a sow to the most beautiful of women, because the affection follows the reason of the species. And amongst men the same thing is seen, according as some resemble one species of brute beast and some another: these having something of the quadruped, and those of birds, and, may be, some affinity, which I will not explain, but through which those have been known who are affected by certain sorts of beasts. Now, it is lawful for the mind which finds itself oppressed by the material conjunction of the soul, to raise itself to the contemplation of another state, to which the soul may arrive, comparing the two, and so through the future despise the present. If a beast had a sense of the difference which exists between his own condition and that of man, and the meanness of his own state with the nobility of the human state, which he would deem it not impossible to be able to reach, he would love death, which would open to him that road, more than that life which keeps him in the present state of being. When the soul complains, saying, "Ah! dogs of Actæon!" she is represented as a thing which appears only in the inferior powers, and against which the mind rebels for having taken away the heart with it; that is to say, the entire affections, with all the army of the thoughts. So that, having a knowledge of the present state, and being ignorant of every other, and not believing that others exist about which she can have any knowledge, she complains of her thoughts, which, tardily turning towards her, come rather to draw her up than, to make themselves accepted by her. And through the distraction which she endures on account of the ordinary love of the material and of things intelligible, she feels herself lacerated and mangled, so that at last she is forced to yield to the more vigorous impulse. And if, by virtue of contemplation, she rises or is caught up above the horizon of the natural affections, whence with purer eye she learns the difference between the one life and the other, then, vanquished by the lofty thoughts, and, as if dead to the body, she aspires to that which is elevated, and, although alive in the body, she vegetates there as if dead, being present as an animating principle and absent in operative activity; not because she does not act while the body is alive, but that the actions of this mass are intermittent, weak, and, as it were, purposeless.

CIC. Thus a certain theologian, who was said to be transported to the third heaven and enchanted with the view of it, said that what he desired was the dissolution of his body.

TANS. So; first complaining of the heart and quarrelling with the thoughts, she now desires to rise on high with them, and exhibits her regret for the connection and familiarity contracted with corporeal matter, and. says: "Leave me life (corporeal), and do not impede my progress upwards to my native home, to my sun. Leave me now, for no longer do my eyes weep tears; neither because I cannot succour them (the thoughts), nor because I cannot remain divided from my happiness. Leave me, for it is not fit nor possible that these two streams should run without their source, that is, without the heart. I will not, I say, make two rivers of tears here below, while my heart, which is the source of such rivers, is flown away on high with its nymphs, which are my thoughts." Thus, little by little, from dislike and regret, she proceeds to the hatred of inferior things, which she partly shows, saying, When shall this ponderous mass of me dissolve? and that which follows.

CIC. This I understand right well, and also that which you would infer about the principal intention; that is to say, that these are the degrees of the loves, of the affections, and of the enthusiasms, according to the degrees of greater and lesser light, of cognition, and of intelligence.

TANS. Thou understandest rightly. From this thou oughtest to learn that doctrine taken from the Pythagoreans and Platonists, which is, that the soul makes the two progressions of ascent and descent, by the care that it has of itself and of matter; being moved by its own proper love of good, and being urged by the providence of fate.

CIC. But, prythee, tell me briefly what you mean about the soul of the world, if she can neither ascend nor descend?

TANS. If you ask of the world, according to the common signification--that is, in so far as it signifies what is called the universe--I say that, being infinite, it has no dimension or measure, is immobile, inanimate, and without form, notwithstanding it is the place of infinite moving worlds and is infinite space, in which are so many large animals that are called stars. If you ask according to the signification held by the true philosophers--that is, in so far as it signifies every globe, every star, such as this earth, the body of the sun, moon, and others--I say that such soul does not ascend nor descend, but turns in a circle. Thus, being compounded of superior and inferior powers, with the superior it turns round the divinity, and with the inferior, towards the mass of the worlds, which is by it vivified and maintained between the tropics of generation and the corruption of living things in those worlds, serving its own life eternally; because the act of the divine providence, always preserves it with divine heat and light, with the same order and measure, in the ordinary and self-same being.

CIC. I have now heard enough upon this subject.

TANS. It happens then that individual souls come to be influenced differently as to their habits and inclinations, according to the diverse degrees of ascension and descension, and come to display various kinds and orders of enthusiasms, of loves, and of senses, not only in the scale of Nature according to the orders of diverse lives which the soul takes up in different bodies, as is expressly declared by the Pythagoreans, Saduchimi and others, and by implication, Plato, and those who dive more profoundly into it, but still more in the scale of human affections, which has as many degrees as the scale of Nature, for man, in all his powers, displays every species of being.

CIC. Therefore from the affections one may know souls, whether they are going up or down, or whether they are from above or from below, whether they are going on towards becoming beasts or towards divine beings, according to the specific being as the Pythagoreans understood it; or according to the similitude of the affections only, as is commonly believed, the human soul not being able, (so long as it is truly human) to become soul of a brute, as Plotinus and other Platonists well said, on account of the quality of its beginning.

TANS. Now to come to the proposition: From animal enthusiasm, this soul, as described, is promoted to heroic enthusiasm, saying, "When shall it be that I rise up to the height of the object, there to dwell in company with my heart and with my fledglings and his?" This same proposition he continues when he says

24. Destiny, when shall I that mountain mount,
Which, blissful to the high gates bringing, bring,
Where those rare beauties I shall counting, count,
When *he* my pain with comfort comforting,
Who my disjointed members joined,
And leaves my dying powers not dead?
My spirit's rival more than rivalled is
If, far from sin, it unassailed may sail,
If thither tending, it may waiting, wait,
And up with that high object rising, rise,
And if my good alone, alone I take,
For which I sure remove of each defect effect,
And so at last may come to enjoy with joy,
As he who all foretells can tell.

O Destiny! O Fate! O divine immutable Providence! when shall it be that I shall climb that mount--that is, that I may arrive at such altitude of mind, as transporting me shall bring me into those outer and inner courts where I may behold and count those rare beauties? When shall it be, that he will effectually comfort my pain, loosening me from the tightened bonds of those cares in which I find myself, he, who formed and united my members, which before were disunited and disjoined: that is Love; he who has joined together these corporeal parts, which were as far divided as one opposite is divided from another; so that these intellectual powers which, through his action he has extinguished, should not be left quite dead, but be again re-animated and made to aspire on high?

When, I say, will he fully comfort me, and give my powers free and speedy flight, by which means my substance may go and nestle there, where, by my efforts, I may make amends and correct my defects, and where (if I arrive) my spirit will be made effectual or prevail over my rival, because there, no excess will oppose, no opposition overcome, no error assail? Oh! if by force he may arrive there, at that height which he is waiting to reach, he will remain on high, at the elevation of his object, and he will take that good that cannot be comprehended by any other than one, that is, by himself, seeing that every other has it in the measure of his own capacity, and this one alone has it in all its fulness. Then will happiness come to me in that manner which he says, "who all foretells"; that is, at that elevation in which the saying all and the doing all is the same thing; in that manner that he says and does who all foretells, that is, who is sufficient for all things and primary, and whose word and pre-ordaining is the true doing and beginning. This is how, in the scale of things superior and inferior, the affection of Love proceeds, as the intellect or sentiment proceeds from these intelligible or knowable objects, to those, or from those to these.

CIC. Thus the greater number of sages believe that Nature delights in this changeful circulation which is seen in the whirling of her wheel.

Fifth Dialogue

I.

CIC. Now show me how I may be able for myself to consider the conditions of these enthusiasts, through that which appears in the order of the warfare here described.

TANS. Behold how they carry the ensign of their affections or fortunes. Let us leave the consideration of their names and habits; enough that we stand upon the meaning of the undertaking and the intelligibility of the writing, alike that which is put for the form of the body of the figure, as well as that which is mostly put as an elucidation of the undertaking.

CIC. Thus will we do. Here then is the first, who carries a shield divided into four colours, and in the crest is depicted a flame under the head of bronze, from the holes in which, issue in great force a smoky wind, and about it is written: "At regna senserunt tria."

TANS. For the explanation of this I would say: that the fire there is that which heats the globe, inside of it is the water, and it happens that this humid element, being rarefied and attenuated by virtue of the heat, and thus resolved into vapour, it requires much greater space to contain it, therefore if it does not find easy exit, it goes on with extreme force, noise, and destruction to break the vessel; but if it finds space and easy exit, so that it can evaporate, it goes out with less violence, little by little, and, according as the water is resolved into vapour, it is dissipated in puffs into the air. Here is signified the heart of the enthusiast where, by a cleverly planned allurement being caught by the amorous flame, it happens that some of the vital substance sparkles with fire, while some in the form of tearful cries rends the bosom, and some other by the expulsion of gusty sighs agitates the air. Therefore he says: "At regna senserunt tria." Now this "at" supposes a difference, or diversity, or opposite; as one might almost say there exists something which might have the same sense, but has it not, which is very well explained in the following rhymes:

25. From these twin lights of me--a little earth--
My wonted tears stream freely to the sea.

The greedy air receives from out my breast
No niggard part of all that breast contains;
And from my heart the lightnings are unlocked
That rise to heaven, and yet diminish not.
Thus pay I to the air, the sea, the fire,
The tribute of my sighs, my tears, my zeal.
The sea, the air, the fire, accept a part of me,
But my divinity no favour shows.
Unkind she turns away. Near her
My tears find no response;
My voice she will not hear,
Nor pitifully will she turn to note my zeal.

Here the subject matter signified by "earth" is the substance of the enthusiast, which is poured from the twin lights--that is, from the eyes--in copious tears that flow to the sea; he sends forth from his breast into the wide air sighs in a great multitude, and the lightnings from his heart, not like a little spark or a weak flame, which, cooling itself in the air, smokes, and transmigrates into other beings; but, potent and vigorous--rather acquiring from others than losing of its own--it joins its congenial sphere.

CIC. I understand it all. To the next.

II.

TANS. Close by is portrayed one who has on his shield a crest, also divided into four colours. There is a sun whose rays extend to the back of the earth, and there is a legend which says: "Idem semper ubique totum."

CIC. I perceive that the interpretation of it will be difficult.

TANS. The more excellent the meaning the less obvious is it, and you will see that it is unequalled, unique, and not strained. You are to consider that the sun, although with regard to the various regions of the earth he is for each one different as to time, place, and degree, yet in respect of the whole globe as such, he always and in every place accomplishes everything, for in whatever part of the ecliptic he is to be found, he makes winter, summer, autumn, and spring, and makes the whole globe of the earth to receive within itself the aforesaid four seasons; for never is it hot at one side unless it is cold on the other; when it is to us very hot in the tropic of Cancer it is very cold in the tropic of Capricorn; so that for the same reason it is winter in that part when it is summer in this, and to those who are in the middle, it is temperate according to the aspect, vernal or autumnal. So the earth always feels the rains, the winds, the heat, the cold; nor would it be damp here if it were not dry in another part, and the sun would not warm it on this side if it had not already left off warming it on the other.

CIC. Even before you have finished, I understand what you would say. You mean that as the sun gives all the impressions to the earth, and this receives them whole and entire, so the Object of the enthusiast, with its active splendour, makes him the passive subject of tears, which are the waters, of ardours, which are the fires, and of sighs, which are certain vapours, which partake of both, which leave the fire, and go to the waters, or leave the waters and go to the fire.

TANS. This is well explained below.

26. When as the sun towards Capricorn declines,
Then do the rains enrich the streams,
As towards the line he goes, or thence returns,
More felt is each Æolian messenger,
Warming the more with every lengthening day
What time towards burning Cancer he remounts.
And equal to this heat, this cold, this zeal
Are these my tears, my sighs, the ardour that I feel.
My constant sighs, my never waning flames
Are only equal to my tears.
My floods and flames howe'er intense they be,
Are never more so than my sighs;
I burn with fervid heat,
And, firmly fixed, I ever sigh and weep.

Cm. This does not so much declare the meaning of the coat of arms, as the preceding discourse did, but it rather supplements or accompanies that discourse.

TANS. Say, rather, that the figure is latent in the first part, and the legend is well explained in the second; as both the one and the other are very properly signified in the type of the sun and of the earth.

CIC. Pass on to the third.

III.

TANS. The third bears on his shield a naked child, stretched upon the green turf, who rests his head upon his arm, with his eyes turned towards the sky to certain edifices, towers, gardens, and orchards, which are above the clouds, and there is a castle of which the material is fire, and in the middle is the sign inscribed: "Mutuo fulcimur."

CIC. What does that mean?

TANS. It means that enthusiast, signified by the naked child as simple, pure, and exposed to all the accidents of Nature and of fortune, who at the same time by the force of thought, constructs castles in the air, and amongst other things a tower, of which the architect is Love, the material is the amorous fire, and the builder is himself, who says: "Mutuo fulcimur"--that is, I build and uphold you there with my thought, and you uphold me here with hope; you would not be in existence were it not for the imagination and the thought with which I form and uphold you, and I should not be alive were it not for the refreshment and comfort that I receive through your means.

CIC. It is true that there is no fancy so vain and so chimerical that may not be a more real and true medicine for an enthusiastic heart than any herb, mineral, oil, or other sort of thing that Nature produces.

TANS. Magicians can do more by means of faith than physicians by the truth; and in the worst diseases the patients benefit more by believing this or that which the former say, than in understanding that which the latter do. Now let the rhymes be read.

27. Above the clouds in that high place,
When oft with dreaming I am fired,
For comfort and refreshment of my soul
An airy castle from my fires I build,
And if my adverse fate incline awhile,

And without scorn or ire will understand
This lofty grace for which I die,
Oh happy then my pains, happy my death.
The ardour of those flames she does not feel,
Nor is she hindered by those snares
With which, oh boy! thou'rt wont to enslave
And lead into captivity both men and gods;
By pity's hand alone, oh Love,
By showing all my woe, thou shalt prevail.

CIC. He shows that which feeds his fancy and bathes his spirit; yet, inasmuch as he is without courage to explain himself and make known his sufferings, although he is so deeply subjected to that anguish, if it should happen that his hard, uncompromising fate should bend a little (as, in the end, fate must soothe him, by showing itself without scorn or anger for the high object), he would consider no happiness so great, no life so blessed, as in such a case would be his happiness in his woes, and his blessedness in his death.

TANS. And with this he comes to declare to Love that the means by which he will gain access to that breast, is not in the ordinary way by the arms with which he usually captivates men and gods, but only by causing the fiery heart and his troubled spirit, to be laid bare, to obtain sight of which it is necessary that compassion open the way, and introduce him to that secret chamber.

IV.

CIC. What is the meaning of that butterfly which flutters round the flame, and almost burns itself? and what means that legend, "Hostis non hostis?"

TANS. The meaning of the butterfly is not difficult, which, seduced by the fascinations of splendour, goes innocently and amicably to meet its death in the devouring flames. Thus, "hostis" stands written for the effect of the fire; "non hostis" for the inclination of the fly. "Hostis," the fly passively; "non hostis," actively. "Hostis," the flame, through its ardour; "non hostis," through its splendour.

CIC. Now what is that which is written on the tablet?

TANS.:
28. Be it far from me to make complaint of love,
Love, without whom I will not happy be,
And though through him these weary toils I bear.
Yet what is given my will shall not reject.
Be clear the sky or dark, burning or cold,
To that one phoenix e'er the same I'll be,
No fate nor destiny can e'er untie
That knot which death unable is to loose;
To heart, to spirit, and to soul,
No pleasure is, no liberty, no life,
No smile, no rapture, no delight,
So sweet, so grateful, so divine,
As these hard bonds, this death of mine,
To which by fate, by will, by nature I incline.

Here, in the figure, he shows the resemblance between the enthusiast and the butterfly attracted towards the light; in the sonnet, however, he demonstrates rather difference and dissimilarity; as it is commonly believed, that if the butterfly foresaw its destruction, it would fly from the light more eagerly than it now pursues it, and would consider it an evil to lose its life through being absorbed into that hostile fire. But to him (the enthusiast) it is no less pleasing to perish in the flames of amorous ardour than to be drawn to the contemplation of the beauty of that rare splendour, under which, by natural inclination, by voluntary election, and by disposition of fate, he labours, serves, and dies more gaily, more resolutely, and more courageously than under whatsoever other pleasure which may offer itself to the heart, liberty which may be conceded to the spirit, and life which may be discovered in the soul.

CIC. Tell me why he says, "ever the same I'll be?"

TANS. Because it seems suitable to bring forward a reason for his constancy, seeing that the sage does not change with the moon, although the fool does so. Thus he is unique, as the phoenix is unique.

V.

CIC. But what signifies that branch of palm, around which is the legend, "Cæsar adest?"

TANS. Without further talk, all may be understood by that which is written on the tablet:

29. Unconquered victor of Pharsalia,
Though all thy warriors be well-nigh spent,
At sight of thee they rise once more;
Their strength returns, they conquer their proud foes;
So does my love--that equals love of heaven--
Become a living presence through my thoughts;
Thoughts that my haughty soul had killed with scorn,
Love brings again stronger than love himself
Thy presence is enough, oh memory!
These to reanimate in all their strength,
And with imperious sov'reignty they rule
And govern each opposing force.
May I be happy in this governance
And with these bonds, and may that light ne'er cease.

There are times when the inferior powers of the soul--like a vigorous and hostile army, which finds itself in its own country practised, expert, and ready--revolt against the foreign adversary, who comes down from the height of the intelligence to curb the people of the valley and of the boggy plains, where, through the baneful presence of the enemies and of such obstacles as deep ditches, advancing they lose themselves, and would be entirely lost, if there were not a certain conversion towards the splendour of intellectual things through the act of contemplation, by means of which they are converted from inferior degrees to superior ones.

CIC. What degrees are these?

TANS. The degrees of contemplation are like the degrees of light, which exist not at all in the darkness, slightly in shade, more in colours, according to their orders, from one opposite which is black to, the other which is white; but more fully do they exist in the splendour diffused over pure transparent bodies, as in a looking-glass and in the moon, and still more brightly in the rays diffused by the sun, but principally and most brilliantly in the sun itself. Now the perceptive and the affectional powers are ordered in this way; the next following always has affinity for the next preceding, and by means of conversion to that which elevates it, it becomes fortified against the inferior, which lowers it; as the reason, through its conversion to the intellect, is not seduced or vanquished by knowledge or comprehension or by passionate affection, but rather, according to the law of the intellect, it is brought to govern and correct the same. It comes to this, therefore, that when the rational appetite strives against sensual concupiscence, if, by the act of conversion, the intellectual light is presented to the eyes, it causes the above appetite to take up again the lost virtue, and giving fresh strength to the nerves, it alarms and puts to rout the enemy.

CIC. In what manner do you mean that such a conversion takes place?

TANS. With three preparatives, which are noted by the contemplative Plotinus in the book of "Intellectual Beauty;" and, of these, the first is by proposing to conform himself to a divine pattern, diverting the sight from things which stand between him and his own perfection, and which are common to those things which are equal and inferior. The second is by applying himself, with full intention and attention, to superior things. The third is by bringing into captivity to God the whole will and affection: for from this it comes to pass that, without doubt, the divinity will influence him; who is everywhere present, and ready to come to the aid of whosoever turns to Him through the act of the intelligence, and who unreservedly presents himself with the affection of the will.

CIC. It is not then corporeal beauty which can allure such an one?

TANS. No, certes; because in that there is no true nor constant beauty, and for this reason it cannot evoke true nor constant love. That beauty, which is seen in bodies is accidental and transitory, and is like those which are absorbed, changed, and spoiled by the changing of the subject, which very often, from being beautiful, becomes ugly, without any change taking place in the soul. The reason then comprehends the truest beauty, through conversion, to that which makes the beauty of the body, and forms it in loveliness,--it is the soul which has thus built and designed it. Now does the intellect rise still higher, and learns that the soul is incomparably more beautiful than any beauty that may be in bodies; but yet it cannot persuade itself that it is beautiful of itself and primarily, for if it be so, what is the cause of that difference which exists in the quality of souls, by which some are wise, amiable, and beautiful, others stupid, odious, and ugly. We must then raise ourselves to that superior intellect which is beautiful in itself and good in itself. This is that sole supreme captain who alone, placed before the eyes of the militant thoughts, enlivens, encourages, strengthens them, and renders them victorious above the scorn of every other beauty and the repudiation of every other good whatsoever. This is the presence which causes every difficulty to be overcome and all opposition to be subdued.

CIC. I understand it all; but what is the meaning of, "May I be happy in this governance and with these bonds, and may that light not cease."

TANS. He means, and he proves, that every sort of love, the greater its dominion and the surer its hold, the more tight are the bonds, and the more firm the yoke, and the more ardent the flames that are felt, as compared with the ordinary princes and tyrants, who adopt a greater rigour wherever they see they have less hold.

CIC. Go on.

VI.

TANS. Here we see described the idea of a flying phœnix, towards which is turned a boy who is burning in the midst of flames; and there is the legend, "Fata obstant." But in order better to understand it, let us read the tablet

30. Sole bird of the sun, thou wandering phœnix!
That measurest thy days as does the world
With lofty summits of Arabia Felix.
Thou art the same thou wast, but I what I was not:
I through the fire of love, unhappy die;
But thee the sun with his warm rays revives;

Thou burn'st, in one, and I, in every place:
Eros my fire, while thine Apollo gives.
Predestined is the term of thy long life
Short span is mine,
And menaced by a thousand ills.
Nor do I know how I have lived, nor how shall live,
Me does blind fate conduct;
But thou wilt come again, again behold thy light.

From the meaning of these lines, you will see that in the figure is drawn the comparison between the fate of the phœnix and that of the enthusiast; and the legend "Fata obstant," does not signify that the fates are adverse either to the boy, or to the phœnix, or to both; but that the fatal decrees for each are not the same, but are diverse and opposite. The phœnix is that which it was, because the, same matter, by means of the fire, renews itself, and becomes again the body of the phœnix, and the same spirit and soul come to inhabit it. The enthusiast is that which he was not, because the subject, which is a man, was first of some other species, according to innumerable differentiations. So that what the phœnix was, is known, and what it will be, is known; but this subject cannot return, except through many and uncertain means, to invest the same or a similar natural form. Then the phœnix, through the sun's presence, changes death into life, and that other, by the presence of love, transmutes life into death. The one kindles his fire on the aromatic altar, the other finds it ever present with him and carries it wherever he goes. The one again, has certain conditions of a long life; but the other, through the infinite differences of time and innumerable circumstances, has the mutable conditions of a short life. The one kindles with certainty, the other with doubt as to whether he will see the sun again.

CIC. What do you think that this means?

TANS. It means the difference that exists between the lower intellect called the intellect of power, either possible or passive, which is uncertain, multifarious, and multiform, and the higher intellect, which, perhaps, is like that which is said by the Peripatetics to be the lowest of the intelligences, and which exerts an immediate influence over all the individuals of the human species, and is called the active and acting intellect. This special human intelligence which influences all individuals is like the moon, which partakes of no other species but that one alone which always renews itself by the transmutation caused in it by the sun, which is the primal and universal intelligence; but the human intellect, both individual and collective, turns as do the eyes towards innumerable and most diverse objects; whence, according to the infinite degrees which exist, it takes on all the natural forms. Hence it is that this particular intellect may be as enthusiastic, vague, and uncertain, as that universal one is quiet, fixed, and certain, whether as regards the desire or the comprehension. Now therefore, as you may very well perceive for yourself, it means that the nature of the comprehension of sense and its varied appetite, is vague, inconstant, and uncertain, and the conception and definite appetite of the intelligence is firm and stable. This is the difference between sensual love, which has no stability nor discretion as to its object, and intellectual love, which aims only at one, sure and fixed, towards which it turns, through which it is illuminated in its conception, by which, being kindled in its affections, it becomes inflamed and brightened, and is maintained in unity and identity of condition.

VII.

CIC. But what is the meaning of that figure of the sun, with a circle inside and another outside, with the legend "Circuit."

TANS. The meaning of this I am certain I should never have understood if I had not heard it from the designer of it himself. Now you must know that "Circuit" has reference to the movement the sun makes round the circle which is drawn inside and outside, in order to signify that the movement both makes and is made; and hence, as a consequence, the sun is to be found in every part of those circles; so that, if he moves and is moved, and is over the whole circumference of the circle equally, then you find in him both movement and rest.

CIC. This I understood in the dialogues on the infinite universe and the innumerable worlds, where it is declared that the divine wisdom is extremely mobile, as Solomon said, and also that the same is most stable, as all those declare who know. Now go on and make me understand the proposition.

TANS. It means that this sun is not like this one, which is commonly believed to go round the earth with the daily movement in twenty-four hours, and with the planetary movement in twelve months, and by which he causes the four seasons of the year to be felt, according as he is found to be in the four cardinal points of the zodiac; but he is such an one, that, being the ethereal eternity itself, and consequently an entire and complete totality, he contains the winter, the spring, the summer, the autumn, together with the day and the night, for he is all and for all, in all points and places.

CIC. Now apply that which you have said to the figure.

TANS. It being impossible here to design the entire sun in every point of the circle, two circles are delineated; one which contains the sun to signify that the movement is made through him, the other which is contained by the sun to show that he is moved by it.

CIC. But this explanation is not very clear and appropriate.

TANS. Suffice it that it is the clearest and most appropriate that he was able to make. If you can make a better one, you shall have permission to remove this one and put it in its place, for this has only been put in, so that the soul should not be without a body.

CIC. What do you say about that "Circuit?"

TANS. That legend contains all the meaning of the thing in so far as it can be explained, for it means that he turns and is turned, that is to say movement present and accomplished.

CIC. Excellent! And therefore those circles which so ill explain the circumstance of movement and rest, we can say are placed there to signify the circulation only. Thus am I satisfied with the subject and with the form of the heroic device. Now read the lines.

TANS.:

31. Mild are thy rays, oh, Sol! from Taurus sent,

> And from the Lion thy beams mature and burn,
> And when thy light from pungent Scorpion darts
> Transcendent is the ardour of thy flames.
> From fierce Deucalion all is struck with cold,
> Stiffened the lakes and locked the running streams.
> With spring, with summer, autumn, and with winter,
> I warm, I kindle, burn and blaze for ever.
> So ardent my desire,
> The object so supreme for which I burn;
> Glowing and unencumbered I behold,
> And make my lightnings flash unto the stars.
> No moment can I count in all the year
> To change the inexorable cross I bear.

Here observe that the four seasons of the year are signified, not by four movable signs, which are Aries, Cancer, Libra, and Capricorn, but by the four which are called fixed-- namely, Taurus, Leo, Scorpio, and Aquarius, to signify the condition, fervour, and perfection of those seasons. Note further, that in virtue of those apostrophes, which are in the eighth line, you can read: I warm, kindle, burn, blaze; or, be thou warmed, kindled, burning, blazing; or, let him warm, kindle, burn, blaze.

You have further to consider that these are not four synonyms, but four different terms, which signify so many degrees of the effects of the fire which first warms, secondly kindles, thirdly burns, and fourthly blazes or inflames that which it has warmed, kindled, and burnt. And thus are denoted in the enthusiast, desire, attention, study, affection, in which he never for a moment feels any change.

CIC. Why does he put them under the title of a cross?

TANS. Because the object, which is the divine light, is, in this life, more felt as a painful longing than in quiet fruition, because our mind is towards that, as the eyes of night birds to the sun.

CIC. Proceed; for from what you have said I understand all.

VIII.

TANS. On the next crest there is painted a full moon and the legend: "Talis mihi semper ut astro," which means that to the star--that is, to the sun--she is ever such as she here shows herself, full and clear in the entire circumference of the circle, which, in order that you may better understand, I will let you hear that which is written on the tablet.

32. Oh, changeful moon, inconstant moon!
With horns now full, now void, thou wanderest.
Mounting, thy sphere now white now dark appears.
The mountains and the valleys of the north thou brightenest,
And turning by thy dust-encumbered steps,
Thou lightest in the south the Lybian heights.
My moon for my continual pain
Is constant ever, ever full.
So is my star,
Which ever from me takes and nothing gives,
For ever burns and ever shines,
Cruel always yet always beautiful.
This noble light of mine
Torments me still and still delights me.

It seems to me, that it means that his particular intelligence is to the universal intelligence ever the same--that is to say, the one is ever illuminated by the other, over the whole hemisphere; notwithstanding that to the inferior powers, and according to the influence of his actions, it appears now dark, and now more and less clear. Or perhaps it means that his speculative intellect, which is ever invariable in its action, is always turned and affected towards the human intelligence signified by the moon. Because, as this is said to be the lowest of all the stars, and is nearest to us, so the illuminating intelligence of all of us in this state is the last in order of the other intelligences, as Averroes and the more subtle Peripatetics say. That intelligence, in so far as it is not in any act, goes down before, or sets to the potential intellect, or as if so to say, it emerged from the bottom of the occult hemisphere, and showed itself now void, now full, according as it gives more or less light of intelligence. Now its sphere is dark, now light, because sometimes it shows itself as a shadow, a semblance, and a vestige, and sometimes more and more openly: now it declines towards the south, now it mounts towards the north--that is, now it removes farther and farther away, and now it approaches nearer and nearer. But the intellect, active with its continual grief--seeing that it is not through its human condition and nature that it Ends itself so wretched, so opposed, courted, solicited, distracted, and, as it were, torn by the inferior powers--sees its object stable, fixed and constant, and ever full, and in the same splendour of beauty. Thus it ever takes away, in so far as it does not concede, and ever gives, in so far as it concedes. It ever burns in the affection in so far as it shines in thoughts, and is always cruel in withdrawing itself through that which withdraws itself; as it is always beautiful in communication with that to which it presents itself. Always does it torment when it is divided from him by difference of locality, as always it delights him being joined to it by affection.

CIC. Now apply your intelligence to the legend.

TANS. he says then, "talis mihi semper;" that is, because of the continual application of my intellect, my memory, and my will, because, I will remember, understand and desire no other; she is ever the same to me, and in so far as I can understand her, she is entirely present, and is not separated from me by any distraction of my thoughts, nor does she become darkened to me through any want of attention, for there is no thought that can divert me from that light nor any necessity of nature which forces me to a less constant attention; "talis mihi semper" on her side, because she is invariable in substance, in virtue, in beauty, and in effect, towards those things that are constant and invariable towards her. She says further, "ut astro," because in respect of the sum, the illuminator of her, she is ever equally luminous, seeing that she is ever turned equally towards him, and he at the same time diffuses his rays equally. As, physically, this moon that we see with the eyes, although towards the earth she appears now dark, now shining, now more, now less illuminated and illuminating, yet is she ever equally irradiated by the sun, because she always reflects his rays over at least the whole of her hemisphere. So also is the hemisphere of this earth ever equally irradiated, although from the watery surfaces she from time to time sends her splendours unequally to the moon,-- which like innumerable other stars we consider as another earth--in the same manner, she also sends hers to the earth, on account of the periodical changes which both experience in finding themselves now the one, now the other, nearer to the sun.

CIC. How can this intelligence be signified by the moon which lights up the hemisphere?

TANS. All the intelligences are signified by the moon, in so far as they are sharers in act and in power, in so far as they have the light materially and by participation, receiving it from another; I say that, as not being lights of themselves, nor by their own nature, but by reflection from the sun, which is the first intelligence, which is pure and absolute light, as it is also pure and absolute action.

CIC. All those things, then, that are dependent, and are not the first act and cause, are they composed of light and shade, of matter and form, of power and action?

TANS. It is so. Furthermore, this soul of ours, in all its substance, is signified by the moon which shines through the hemisphere of the superior powers, by which it is turned towards the light of the intelligible world, and is dark through the inferior powers, by which it is occupied with material things.

IX.

CIC. It seems to me that what has just been said has some connection and analogy with the impression that I see on the next shield, where stands a gnarled and rugged oak, against which the wind is raging, and it is circumscribed by the legend, "ut robori robur," and here is the tablet, which says:

33. Old oak, that spread'st thy branches to the air,
And firmly in the earth dost fix thy roots;
No shifting of the land, no mighty elements,
Which Heaven from the stormy north unlocks;

Nor whatso'er the gruesome winter sends,
Can tear thee from the spot where thou art chained.
Thou art the veritable portrait of my faith,
Which, fixed, remains 'gainst every casual chance.
Ever the self-same ground dost thou
Grasp, cultivate and comprehend; and stretch
Thy grateful roots unto the generous breast.
Upon one only object I
Have fixed my spirit, sense, and intellect.

TANS. The legend is clear, by which the enthusiast boasts of having the strength and vigour of the oak, and as before said of being ever the same in respect to the one only phoenix, and in the next preceding one, conforming himself to that moon which ever shines so brightly and is so beautiful, and also in that he does not resemble this antichthon between our earth and the sun in so far as it changes to our eyes, but in that it ever receives within itself an equal amount of the solar splendour, and through this remains constant and firm against the rough winds and tempests of winter, through the stability that he has in his star, in which he is planted by affection and intention, as the roots of the oak twist and weave themselves into the veins of the earth.

CIC. I hold it better worth living in quiet and without vexation than to be forced to endure so much.

TANS. That is a maxim of the Epicureans which, being well understood, would not be considered so unworthy as the ignorant hold it to be, seeing that it does not detract from what I have called virtue, nor does it impair the perfection of firmness, but it rather adds to that perfection as it is understood by the vulgar, for Epicurus does not hold that, a true and complete strength and firmness which feels and bears inconveniences, but that which bears them and feels them not. He does not consider him perfect in divine heroic love, who feels the spur, the, cheek, or remorse or trouble about other love; but him who has no feeling of other affections; so that being fixed in one pleasure, there is no displeasure that has any power to jostle him c,. dislodge him from his place. And this it is to touch the highest blessedness of this state, to have rapture and no sense of pain.

CIC. The ignorant do not believe in this meaning of Epicurus.

TANS. Because they neither read his own books, nor those that report his maxims without invidiousness, but there are those who read the course of his life and the conditions of his death, where with these words he dictated the beginning of his testament: "Being in the last, and at the same time, the happiest day of our life, we have ordained this with a healthy, tranquil mind at rest; for whatever acute sorrow may torment us from one side, that torment is entirely annulled by the pleasure of our own inventions and the consideration of our end." And it is manifest that he no longer felt more pleasure than sorrow in eating, drinking, repose, and in generating, but in not feeling hunger, nor thirst, nor fatigue, nor sensuality. From this may be understood what is according to us the perfection of firmness; not in this, that the tree neither bends nor breaks, nor is rent, but in that it does not so much as stir, and its prototype keeps spirit, sense, and intellect, fixed there, where the shock of the tempest is not felt.

CIC. Do you then think it is a thing to be desired, to bear shocks in order to prove that you are strong?

TANS. You say "to bear;" and this is a part of firmness, but it is not the whole of that virtue, which consists in bearing strongly, as I say, or in not feeling, as Epicurus said. Now this loss of feeling is caused by being entirely absorbed in the cultivation of virtue, or of real good and felicity, in such wise that Regulus did not feel the chest, Lucretia the dagger, Socrates the poison, Anaxagoras the mortar, Scævola the fire, Cocles the abyss, and other worthies felt not those things which would torment and fill with terror the vulgar crowd.

CIC. Now pass on.

X.

TANS. Look at this other who bears the device of an anvil and a hammer, round which is the legend "ab Aetna!" But here Vulcan is introduced:

34. Not now to my Sicilian mount I turn,
Where thou dost forge the thunderbolts of Jove,

> Here, rugged Vulcan will I stay;
> Here, where a prouder giant moves,
> Who burns and rages against Heaven in vain,
> Soliciting new cares and divers trials.
> Here is a better smith and Mongibello
> A better anvil, better forge and hammer;
> For here behold a bosom full of sighs,
> Which blows the furnace and the fire revives.
> The soul nor yields nor bends to these rough blows,
> But bears exulting this long martyrdom,
> And makes a harmony from these sharp pangs.

Here are shown the pains and troubles which beset love, principally love of a low kind, which is no other than the forge of Vulcan, that smith who makes the bolts of Jove which torment offending souls.

For ill-ordered love has in itself the beginning of its own pain, seeing that there is a God near us, in us, and with us. There is in us a certain sacred mind and intelligence, which supplies an affection of its own, which has its own avenger, which, through remorse for certain shortcomings, flagellates the transgressing spirit as with a hammer. It notes our actions and our affections, and as it is treated by us, so are we treated by it. In every lover I say there is this smith Vulcan, and as there is no man that has not a god within him, so there is no lover that has not a god within him, and no lover within whom this god is not. Most certainly there is a god in every man, but what god it is in each one is not so easy to know. And even though we should examine and distinguish, yet do I believe that none other than Love could declare it, he being the one who pulls the oars, and fills the sails, and modifies this compound, so that it comes to be well or ill affected. I say well or ill affected as to that which it puts in execution through the moral actions and through contemplation; for the rest, all lovers are apt to experience some difficulties, things being as they are, so entangled; there being no good whatever, either of conception or of the affections, which is not joined to or stands in opposition to evil, as there is no truth which is not joined or opposed to what is false, so there is no love without fear, ardour, jealousy, rancour, and other passions, which proceed from their opposites, and which disturb us, as the other opposite causes satisfaction. Thus the soul striving to recover its natural beauty seeks to purify itself, to heal itself, and to reform itself, and to this end it uses fire, because, being like gold, mixed with earth and crude, with a certain rigour it tries to liberate itself from defilement, and this result is obtained when the intellect, the real smith of Jove, puts itself to the work and causes an active exercise of the intellectual powers.

CIC. It seems to me that this is referred to in the "Banquet" of Plato, where it says that Love has inherited from his mother, Poverty, that dried-up, thin, pale, bare-footed, and submissive condition without a home, without anything, and through these is signified the torture of the soul that is torn with contrary affections.

TANS. So it is; because the spirit, full of this enthusiasm, becomes absorbed in profound thoughts, stricken with urgent cares, kindled with fervent desires, excited by frequent crises: whence the soul, finding itself in suspense, becomes less diligent and active in the government of the body through the acts of the vegetative power; thus the body becomes lean, ill-nourished, attenuated, poor in blood, and rich in melancholy humours, and these, if they do not administer to the disciplined soul, or to a clear and lucid spirit, may lead to insanity, folly, and brutal fury, or at least to a certain disregard of self, and a contempt of its own being, which is symbolized by Plato in the bare feet. Love becomes subjected and flies suddenly down to earth when it is attached to low things, but flies high when it is fixed upon more worthy enterprises. In conclusion, whatever love it may be, it is ever afflicted and tormented in such a way that it cannot fail to supply material for the forge of Vulcan; because the soul, being a divine thing, and by nature, not a servant but the mistress of corporeal matter, she becomes troubled in that she voluntarily serves the body, wherein she finds nothing to satisfy her, and albeit, fixed in the thing loved, yet now and then she becomes agitated, and fluctuates amidst the waves of hope, fear, doubt, ardour, conscience, remorse, determination, repentance, and other scourges, which are the bellows, the coals, the forge, the hammer, the pincers, and other instruments which are found in the workshop of the sordid grimy consort of Venus.

CIC. Enough has been said upon this subject. Let us see what follows.

XI.

TANS. Here is a golden apple, rich with various kinds of precious enamel, and there is a legend about it which says, "Pulchriori detur."

CIC. The allusion to the fact of the three goddesses who submitted themselves to the judgment of Paris is very common. But read the lines which more specifically disclose the meaning of the present enthusiast.

TANS.:
35. Venus, the goddess of the third heaven
(Mother of the archer blind, who conquers all),
She whose father is the head of Zeus,
And Juno, most majestic wife of Jove,
These call the Trojan shepherd to be judge,
And to the fairest give the ruddy sphere.
Compared with Venus, Pallas, and the Queen of Heaven,
My perfect goddess bears away the palm.
The Cyprian queen may boast her royal limbs,
Minerva charm with her transcendent wit,
And Juno with a majesty supreme;
But she who holds my heart all these excels
In wisdom, majesty, and loveliness.

Here he makes a comparison between his object (or ideal) which comprises all circumstances, all conditions, and all kinds of beauty, in one subject, and others which exhibit each only one, and that through various hypotheses, as with corporeal beauty, all the conditions of which Apelles could not find in one, but in many virgins. Now here, where there are three kinds of the beautiful, although it seems that all of these exist in each of the three goddesses--Venus not being found wanting in wisdom and majesty, Juno not lacking loveliness and wisdom, and Pallas being full of majesty and beauty, in each case it is a fact that one quality exceeds the others, so that it comes to be held as distinctive of the one, and the other as incidental to all, seeing that of those three gifts, one predominates in each and proclaims her sovereign over the others. And the cause of this difference lies in the fact of possessing these qualities, not primarily and in their essence, but by participation and derivation; as in all things which are dependent, their perfection depends upon the degrees of major and minor and more and less. But in the simplicity of the divine essence, all exists in totality, and not according to any measure, and therefore wisdom is not greater than beauty and majesty, and goodness is not greater than strength: not only are all the attributes equal, they are one and the same thing. As in the sphere all the dimensions are not only equal, the length being equal to the depth and breadth, but are also identical, seeing that what in a sphere is called deep, may also be called long and wide. Likewise is it, as to height in divine wisdom, which is the same as the depth of power and the breadth of goodness. All these perfections are equal, because they are infinite. Of necessity, one is according to the sum of the other, seeing that where things are finite it may result in this, that it is more wise than beautiful or good, more good and beautiful than wise, more wise and good than powerful, and more powerful than good or wise. But where there is infinite wisdom there cannot be other than infinite power, otherwise there would be no infinite knowledge. Where there is infinite goodness there must be infinite wisdom, otherwise there would be no infinite goodness. Where there is infinite power there must be infinite goodness and wisdom, because there is the being able to know and the, knowing to be able. Now, observe how the object of this enthusiast, who is, as it were, inebriated with the drink of the gods, is incomparably higher than others which are different. I mean to say that the divine essence comprehends in the very highest degree perfection of all kinds, so that according to the degree in which this particular form may have participated, he can understand all, do all, and be such an attached friend to one that he may come to feel contempt and indifference towards every other beauty. Therefore to her should be consecrated the spherical apple as to her who seems to be all in all; not to Venus, who is beautiful but is surpassed in wisdom by Minerva, and by Juno in majesty; not to Pallas than whom Venus is more beautiful, and the other more magnificent; not to Juno, who is not the goddess of intelligence or of love.

CIC. Truly, as are the degrees of Nature and of the essences, so in proportion are the degrees of the intelligible orders and the glories of the amorous affections and enthusiasms.

XII.

CIC. The following bears a head with four faces, which blow towards the four corners of the heavens, and are four winds in one subject; above these stand two stars, and in the centre the legend "Novae ortae aeoliae." I would like to know what that signifies.

TANS. I think that the meaning of this device is consequent upon that which precedes it, for, as there the object is declared to be infinite beauty, so here is proposed what may be called a similar aspiration, study, affection, and desire. I believe that these winds are set to signify sighs; but this we shall see when we come to read the lines:

36. Sons of the Titan Astræus and Aurora,
Who trouble heaven, earth, and the wide sea,
Leave now this stormy war of elements,
And fight anon with the high gods.
No more in my Æolian caves ye dwell,
No more does my restraining power compel;
But caught are ye and closed within that breast,
With moans and sobs and bitter sighs opprest.
Turbulent brothers of the stars,
Companions of the tempests of the seas,
Those lights are all that may avail
Peace to restore; murderous yet innocent;
Which, open or concealed,
Will bless with calm, or curse with pride.

Evidently, here, Æolus is introduced as speaking to the winds, which he declares are no longer tempered by him in the Æolian caverns, but by two stars in the breast of this enthusiast. Here, the two stars do not mean the two eyes which are in the forehead, but the two appreciable kinds of divine beauty and goodness, of that infinite splendour, which so influences intellectual and rational desire, that it brings him to a condition of infinite aspiration, according to the way and the degree with which he comes to comprehend that glorious light. For love, while it is finite, contented, and fixed in a certain measure, is not in the form of the species of divine beauty, but as it goes on with ever higher aspirations, it may be said to verge towards the infinite.

CIC. How is breathing, made to mean aspiring? What relation has desire with the winds?

TANS. Whosoever in this present condition aspires, also sighs, and the same breathes; and therefore the vehemence of the aspiration is noted by the hieroglyph of strong breathing.

CIC. But there is a difference between sighing and breathing.

TANS. Therefore it is not put as if one stood for the other, or as being identical, but as being similar.

CIC. Go on then with our proposition.

TANS. The infinite aspiration then, indicated by the sighs and symbolized by the winds, is not under the dominion of Æolus in the Æolic caverns, but of the aforementioned two lights, which are, not only blameless, but benevolent in killing the enthusiast, inasmuch as they cause him to die to every other thing, except the absorbing affection; at the same time, they, being closed and concealed, render him unquiet, and being open, they will tranquillize him, because at this time, when the eyes of the human mind in this body are covered with a nebulous veil, the soul, through such studies, becomes troubled and harassed, and he being thus torn and goaded, will attain only that amount of quiet as will satisfy the condition of his nature.

CIC. How can our finite intellect follow after the infinite ideal?

TANS. Through the infinite potency it possesses.

CIC. This would be useless, if ever it came into effect.

TANS. It would be useless, if it had to do with a finite action, where infinite potency would be wanting, but not with the infinite action where infinite potency is positive, perfection.

CIC. If the human intellect is finite in nature and in act, how can it have an infinite potency?

TANS. Because it is eternal, and in this ever has delight, so that it enjoys happiness without end or measure; and because, as it is finite in itself, so it may be infinite in the object.

CIC. What difference is there between the infinity of the object and the infinity of the potentiality?

TANS. This is finitely infinite, and that infinitely infinite. But to return to ourselves. The legend there says: "Novae Liparææ æoliæ," because it seems as if we are to believe that all the winds which are in the abysmal caverns of Æolus were converted into sighs, if we include those which proceed from the affection, which aspires continually to the highest good and to the infinite beauty.

XIII.

CIC. Here we see the signification of that burning light around which is written: "Ad vitam; non ad horam."

TANS. Persistence in such a love and ardent desire of true goodness, by which in this temporal state the enthusiast is consumed. This, I think, is shown in the following tablet

34. What time the day removes the orient vault,
The rustic peasant leaves his humble home,
And when the sun with fiercer tangent strikes,
Fatigued and parched, he sits him in the shade;
Then plods again with hard, laborious toil,
Until black night the hemisphere enshrouds.
And then he rests. But I must ever chafe
At morning, noon-day, evening, and at night.
These fiery rays
Which stream from those two arches of my sun,
Ne'er fade from the horizon of my soul.
So wills my fate;
But blazing every hour

From their meridian they burn the afflicted heart.

CIC. This tablet expresses with greater truth than perspicacity the sense of the figure.

TANS. It is not necessary for me to make any effort to point out to you the appropriateness, as it only requires a little attentive consideration. The rays of the sun are the ways in which the divine beauty and goodness manifest themselves to us; and they are fiery because they cannot be comprehended by the intellect without at the same time kindling the affections. The two arches of the sun are the two kinds of revelation, that scholastic theologians call early and late, whence our illuminating intelligence, as an airy medium, deduces that species, either in virtue, which it contemplates in itself, or in efficacy, which it beholds in its effects. The horizon of the soul, in this place, is that part of the superior potentialities where the vigorous impulse of the affection comes to aid the lively comprehension of the intellect, being signified by the heart, which, burning at all hours, torments itself; because all those fruits of love that we can gather in this state are not so sweet that they have not united with them a certain affliction, which proceeds from the fear of imperfect fruition: as especially occurs in the fruits of natural affection, the condition of which I cannot do better than explain in the words of the Epicurean poet:

Ex hominis vera facie, pulchroque colore
Nil datur in corpus præter simulacra fruendum
Tenuia, quæ vento spes captat sæpe misella.
Ut bibere in somnis sitiens cum quærit, et humor
Non datur, ardorem in membris qui stinguere possit,
Sed laticum simulacra petit, frustraque laborat,
In medioque sitit torrenti flumine potans:
Sic in amore Venus simulacris ludit amantis,
Nec satiare queunt spectando corpora coram,
Nec manibus quicquam teneris abradere membris
Possunt, errantes incerti corpore toto.
Denique cum membris conlatis flore fruuntur,
Ætatis, dum jam præsagit gaudia corpus,
Atque in eo est Venus, ut muliebria conserat arva,
Adfigunt avide corpus, iunguntque salivas

Oris, et inspirant pressantes dentibus ora,
Necquiquam, quoniam nihil inde abradere possunt,
Nec penetrare, et abire in corpus corpore tote.

In the same way, he judges as to the kind of taste that we can have of divine things, which, while we force ourselves to penetrate, and unite with them, we find that we have more pain in the desire than pleasure in the realization. And this may have been the reason why that wise Hebrew said that he who increases knowledge increases pain; because from the greater comprehension grows the greater desire. And this is followed by greater vexation and grief for the deprivation of the thing desired. So the Epicurean, who led a most tranquil life, said opportunely:

Sed fugitare decet simulacra, et pabula amoris
Abstergere sibi, atque alio convertere mentem,
Nec servare sibi curam certumque dolorem:
Ulcus enim virescit, A inveterascit alendo,
Inque dies gliscit furor, atque ærumna gravescit.
Nee Veneris fructu caret is, qui vitat amorem,
Sed potius, quæ sunt, sine poena, commoda sumit.

CIC. What is meant by the meridian of the heart?

TANS. That part or region of the will which is highest and most exalted, and where it becomes most strongly, clearly, and effectually kindled. He means that such affection is not as in its beginning, where it stirs, nor as at the end, where it reposes, but as in the middle, where it becomes fervid.

XIV.

CIC. But what means that glowing arrow, which has flames in place of a hard point, around which is encircled a noose with the legend: "Amor instat ut instans"? Say, what does it mean?

TANS. It seems to me to mean that love never leaves him, and at the same time eternally afflicts him.

CIC. I see the noose, the arrow, and the fire. I understand that which is written: "Amor instat"; but that which follows I cannot understand--that is, that love as an instant, or persisting, persists; which has the same poverty of idea as if one said:

"This undertaking he has feigned as a feint; he bears it as he bears it, understands it as he understands it, values it as he values it, and esteems it as he who esteems it."

TANS. It is easy for him to decide and condemn who does not even consider. That "instans" is not an adjective from the verb "instare," but it is a noun substantive used for the instant of time.

CIC. Now, what is the meaning of the phrase "love endures as an instant?"

TANS. What does Aristotle mean in his book on Time, when he says that eternity is an instant, and that all time is no more than an instant?

CIC. How can this be, seeing that there is no time so short that it cannot be divided into seconds? Perhaps he would say that in one instant there is the Flood, the Trojan war, and we who exist now; I should like to know how this instant is divided into so many centuries and years, and whether, by the same rule, we might not say that the line is a point?

TANS. If time be one, but in different temporal subjects, so the instant is one in different and all parts of time. As I am the same I was, am, and shall be; so I myself am always the same in the house, in the temple, in the field, and wheresoever I am.

CIC. Why do you wish to make out that the instant is the whole of time?

TANS. Because if it were not an instant, it would not be time; therefore time in essence and substance is no other than an instant, and let this suffice, if you understand it, because I do not intend to perorate upon the entire physics; so that you must understand that he means to say that the whole of love is no less present than the whole of time; because this "instans" does not mean a moment of time.

CIC. This meaning must be specified in some way, if we do not wish to see the motto invalidated by equivocation, by which we are free to suppose that he meant to say that his love was but for an instant--that is, for an atom of time, and of nothing more, or that he means that it is as you interpret it, everlasting.

TANS. Surely, if these two contrary meanings were implied, the legend would be nonsense. But it is not so, if you consider well, for it cannot be that in one instant, which is an atom or point, love persists or endures; therefore one must of necessity understand the instant in another signification. And for the sake of getting out of the mesh, read the stanza:

38. One time scatters and one gathers;
One builds, one breaks; one weeps, one laughs;
One time to sadness, one to gaiety inclines;
One labours and one rests; one stands, one sits;
One proffers and one takes away;
One stays and one removes; one animates, one kills.
In all the years, the months, the days, the hours,
Love waits on me, strikes, binds, and burns.
To me continual dissolution,
Continual weeping holds me and destroys.
All times to me are full of woe;
All things time takes from me,
And gives me naught, not even death.

CIC. I understand the meaning quite perfectly, and confess that all things agree very well. It is time to proceed to the next.

XV.

TANS. Here behold a serpent languishing in the snow, where a labourer has thrown it, and a naked child burning in the midst of the fire, with certain other details and circumstances, with the legend which says: "Idem, itidem non idem." This seems more like an enigma than anything else, and I do not feel sure that I can explain it at all; yet I do believe that it means that the same fate vexes, and the same torments both the one and the other--that is, immeasurably, without mercy and unto death, by means of various instruments or contrary principles, showing itself the same whether cold or hot. But this, it seems to me, requires longer and special consideration.

CIC. Some other time. Read the lines:

39. Limp snake, that writhest in the snow,

Twisting and turning here and there
To find some ease from the tormenting cold,
If the congealing ice could know thy pain,
Or had the sense to feel thy smart,
And thou couldst find a voice for thy complaint,
I do believe thy argument would make it pitiful.
I with eternal fire am scourged, am burnt, and bitten,
And in the iciness of my divinity find no deliverance,
No pity does she feel, nor can she know, alas!
The rigorous ardour of my flames.
40. Serpent, thou fain wouldst flee, but canst not
Try for thy hiding-place, it is no more;
Recall thy strength, 'tis spent;
Wait for the sun, behind thick fog he hides;
Cry mercy of the hind, he fears thy tooth.
Fortune invoke, she hears thee not, the jade!
Nor flight, nor place, nor star, nor man, nor fate
Can bring to thee deliverance from death.
Thou dost become congealed. Melting am I.
I like thy rigours, thee my ardour pleases;
Help have I none for thee, and thou hast none for me.
Clear is our evil fate--all hope resign.

CIC. Let us go, and by the way we will seek to untie this knot--if possible.

TANS. So be it.

THE APOLOGY OF THE NOLAN TO THE MOST VIRTUOUS AND LOVELY LADIES.

O LOVELY, graceful nymphs of England!
Not in repugnance nor in scorn,
Our spirit holds you, Nor would our pen abase you
More than it must--to call you feminine!
Exemption I am sure you would not claim
Being subject to the common influence;
Shining on earth as do the stars in heaven.
Your sov'reign beauty, ladies, our austerity
Cannot depreciate, nor would do so,
For we have not in view a superhuman kind.
Such poison, therefore, far from you be set,
For here we see the one, the great Diana,
Who is to you as sun amongst the stars.
Wit, words, learning and art,
And whatsoe'er is mine of scribbling faculty,
I humbly place before you.

THE
HEROIC ENTHUSIASTS

(*GLI EROICI FURORI*)

An Ethical Poem

By
GIORDANO BRUNO

PART THE SECOND

PREFACE.

THE second part of "The Heroic Enthusiasts" which I am now sending to the press is on the same subject as the first, namely the struggles of the soul in its upward progress towards purification and freedom, and the author makes use of lower things to picture and suggest the higher. The aim of the Heroic Enthusiast is to get at the Truth and to see the Light, and. he considers that all the trials and sufferings of this life, are the cords which draw the soul upwards, and the spur which quickens the mind and purifies the will.

The blindness of the soul may signify the descent into the material body, and "visit the various kingdoms" may be an allusion to the soul passing through the mineral, vegetable, and animal kingdoms before it arrives at man.

It is interesting to note that in the first part of "The Heroic Enthusiasts", Bruno makes a distinct allusion to the power of steam, and in the second part, one might almost think, that in using the number nine in connexion with the blind men, he intended a reference to electricity, for we read in "The Secret Doctrine," by H. P. Blavstsky, "There exists an universal *agent unique*, of all forms and of life, that is called Od, Ob, and Aour, active and passive, positive and negative, like clay and night; it is the first light in creation; the first light of the primordial Elo-him--the A-dam,-male and female, or, (scientifically) Electricity and Life. Its universal value is nine, for it is the ninth letter of the alphabet and the ninth door of the fifty portals or gateways, that lead to the concealed mysteries of being. . . . Od is the pure life-giving Light or magnetic fluid."

The notices of the press upon the first half of this work, were for the most part such, as to lead me to hope that the appearance of the second part will meet with a favourable reception.

When I first began this translation little was known about Giordano Bruno except through the valuable works of Sig. Berti and Sig. Levi, and since then Mrs. Firth has given us a life of the Nolan, written in English, and several able articles in the magazines have been published, in one of which, by C.

E. Plumptre (*Westminster Review*, August, 1889), an interesting parallel is drawn between Shelley and Bruno.

I will close this short notice with a sentence from an article in the *Nineteenth Century*, September, 1889, entitled "Criticism as a trade." "There is probably no author who does not feel how much he owes to the writers who have reviewed his books, whether he has occasion to acknowledge it or not. It is humiliating to find how many errors remain in writings that seemed comparatively free from them. Everyone who knows his subject, and has any modesty, is aware that there are defects in his work which his own eye has not seen; and he is more than grateful for the correction of every error that is pointed out to him by an honest censor." If this is the case with authors who produce original work, it may be still more aptly said of translators, especially of those who attempt to translate books so full of difficulties as those presented in the works of Giordano Bruno.

L. WILLIAMS.

SECOND PART OF THE
HEROIC ENTHUSIASTS.
First Dialogue.

Interlocutors: CESARINO. MARICONDO.

I.

CES. It is said that the best and most excellent things are in the world when the whole universe responds from every part, perfectly, to those things; and this it is said takes place as the planets arrive at Aries, being when that one of the eighth sphere again reaches the upper invisible firmament, where is also the other Zodiac; and low and evil things prevail when the opposite disposition and order supervene, and thus through the power of change comes the continual mutation of like and unlike, from one opposite to another. The revolution then of the great year of the world is that space of time in which, through the most diverse customs and, effects, and. by the most opposite and contrary means, it returns to the same again. As we see in particular years such as that of the sun, where the beginning of an opposite tendency is the end. of one year, and the end of this is the beginning of that. Therefore now that we have been in the dregs of the sciences, which have brought forth the dregs of opinions, which are the cause of the dregs of customs and, of works, we may certainly expect to return to the better condition.

MARICONDO. Know, my brother, that this succession and order of things is most true and most certain; but as regards ourselves in all ordinary conditions whatever, the present afflicts more than the past, nor can these two together console, but only the future, which is always in hope and expectation as you may see designated in this figure which is taken from the ancient Egyptians, who made a certain statue which is a bust, upon which they placed three heads, one of a wolf which looks behind, one of a lion with the face turned half round, and the third of a dog who looks straight before him; to signify that things of the past afflict by means of thoughts, but not so much as things of the present which actually torment, while the future ever promises something better; therefore behold the wolf that howls, the lion that roars and the dog that barks (applause).

CES. What means that legend that is written above?

MAR. See, that above the wolf is Lam, above the lion Modo, above the dog Praeterea, which are words signifying the three parts of time.

CES. Now read the tablet.

MAR. I will do so.

41. A wolf, a lion, and a dog appear
At dawn, at midday, and dark night.
That which I spent, retain and for myself procure,
So much was given, is given, and may be given;
For that which I did, I do, and have to do.
In the past, in the present and in the future,
I do repent, torment myself and re-assure,
For the loss, in suffering and in expectation.
With sour, with bitter and with sweet
Experience, the fruits, and hope,
Threatens, afflict, and comforts me.
The age I lived, do live and am to live,
Affrights me, shakes me and upholds
In absence, presence and in prospect.
Much, too much and sufficient
Of the past, of now, and of to come,
Pat me in fear, in anguish and in hope.

CES. This is precisely the humour of a furious lover, though the same may be said of nearly all mortals who are seriously affected in any way. We cannot say that this accords with all conditions in a general way, but only with those mortals who were, and who are, wretched. So that to him who sought a kingdom and obtained it, belongs the fear of losing the same; and to one who has laboured to secure the fruits of love, such as the special grace of the beloved, belongs the tooth of jealousy and suspicion. Thus, too, with the states of the world; when we find ourselves in darkness and in adversity we may surely prophecy light and prosperity, and when we are in a state of happiness and discipline, doubtless we have to expect the advent of ignorance and distress. As in the case of Hermes Trismegistus, who, seeing Egypt in all the splendour of the sciences and of occultism, so that he considered that men were consorting with gods and spirits and were in consequence most pious, he made that prophetic lament to Asclepios, saying that the darkness of new religions and cults must follow, and that of the then present things nothing would remain but idle tales and matter for condemnation. So the Hebrews, when they were slaves in Egypt, and banished to the deserts, were comforted by their prophets with the hope of liberty and the reacquisition of their country; when they were in authority and tranquillity they were menaced with dispersion and captivity. And as in these days there is no evil nor injury to which we are not subject, so there is no good nor honour that we may not promise ourselves. Thus does it happen to all the other generations and states, the which, if they endure and be not destroyed entirely by the force of vicissitude, it is inevitable that from evil they come to good, from good to evil, from low estate to high, from high to low, out of obscurity into splendour, out of splendour into obscurity, for this is the natural order of things; outside of which order, if another should be found which destroys or corrects it, I should believe it and not dispute it, for I reason with none other than a natural spirit.

MAR. We know that you are not a theologian but a philosopher, and that you treat of philosophy and not of theology.

CES. It is so. Bat let us see what follows.

II.

CES. I see a smoking thurible, supported by an arm, and the legend which says: "Illius aram," and then the following:--

42. Now who shall. say the breath of my desire
Of high and holy worship is demeaned

If decked in divers forms ornate she come
Through vows I offer to the shrine of Fame?
And if another work should call, and lead me on,
Who would aver that more it might beseem
If that, of Heaven so loved and eulogized,
Should hold me not in its captivity.
Leave, oh leave me, every other wish,
Cease, fretting thoughts, and give me peace;
Why draw me forth from looking at the sun,
From looking at the sun that I so love.
You ask in pity, wherefore lookest thou
On that, on which to look is thy undoing?
Wherefore so captivated by that light?
And I will say, because to me this pain
Is dearer than all other pleasures are.

    MAR. In reference to this I told you that although one should be attached to corporeal and external beauty yet he may honourably and worthily be so attached; provided that, through this material beauty, which is a glittering ray of spiritual form and action, of which it is the trace and shadow, he comes to raise himself to the consideration and worship of divine beauty, light and majesty; so that, from these visible things his heart becomes exalted towards those things which are more excellent in themselves and grateful to the purified soul, in so far as they are removed from matter and sense. Ah me! he will say, if beauty so shadowy, so dim, so fugitive, painted on the surface of bodily matter pleases me so much, and moves my affections so much, and stamps upon my spirit I know not what of reverence for majesty, captivates me, softly binds me, and draws me, so that I find nothing that comes within the senses that satisfies me so much,--how will it be with the substantially, originally, primitively beautiful? How will it be with my soul, the divine intellect, and the law of nature? It is right, then, that the contemplation of this vestige of light lead me, through the purification of my soul, to the imitation, and to conformity and participation in that which is more worthy, and higher, into which I am transformed and unto which I unite myself: for I am certain that nature, which has placed this beauty before my eyes and has gifted me with an interior sense, through which I am able to infer a deeper and incomparably greater beauty, wills that I be promoted to the altitude and eminence of more excellent kinds. Nor do I believe that my true divinity, as she shows herself to me in symbols and vestiges, will worn me if in symbols and vestiges I honour her and sacrifice to her; as my heart and affections are always so ordered as to look higher. For who may he be, that can honour in essence and real substance, if in such manner he cannot understand it?

It is in and through Symbols that man, consciously or unconsciously, lives, works, and has his being. For is not a Symbol ever, to him who has eyes for it, some dimmer or clearer revelation of the Godlike?--("Sartor Resartus.")

CES. Right well do you demonstrate how, to men of heroic, spirit, all things turn to good and how they are able to turn captivity into greater liberty, and the being vanquished into an occasion for greater victory. Well dost thou know that the love of corporeal beauty to those who are well disposed, not only does not keep them back from higher enterprises, but rather does it lend wings to arrive at these, when the necessity for love is converted into a study of the virtuous, through which the lover is forced into those conditions in which he is worthy of the thing loved and perchance of even a still higher, better and more beautiful thing; so that be comes to be either contented to have gained that which he desires, or so satisfied with its own beauty, that he can despise that of others, which comes to be, by him, vanquished and overcome, so that he either remains tranquil, or else he aspires to things more excellent and grand. And so will the heroic spirit ever go on trying until it becomes raised to the desire of divine beauty itself, without similitude, figure, symbol, or kind, if it be possible, and what is more one knows that he will reach that height.

MAR. You see, Cesarino, how this enthusiast is justified in his anger against those who reproach him with being in captivity to a low beauty, to which he dedicates his vows, and attributes these forms, so that he is deaf to those voices which call him to nobler enterprises: for these low things are derived from those, and are dependent upon them, so that through these you may gain access to those, according to their own degrees. These, if they be not God, are things divine, are living images of Him, in the which, if He sees Himself adored, He is not offended. For we have a charge from the supernal spirit which says: Adorate sgabellum pedum eius. And in another place a divine messenger says: Adorabimus ubi steterunt pedes eius.

CES. God, the divine beauty, and splendour shines and *is* in all things; and therefore it does not appear to me an error to admire Him in all things, according to the way in which we have communion with them. Error it would surely be if we should give to another the honour due to Him alone. But what means the enthusiast when he says, "Leave, leave me, every other wish"?

MAR. That he banishes every thought presented to him by different objects, which have not the power to move him and which would rob him of the sight of the sun which comes to him through that window more than through others.

CES. Why, importuned by thoughts, does he continually gaze at that splendour which destroys him, and yet does not satisfy him, as it torments him ever so fiercely?

MAR. Because all our consolations in this state of controversy are not without their discouragements, however vast those consolations may be just as the fear of a king for the loss of his kingdom, is greater than that of a mendicant who is in peril of losing ten farthings; and more important is the care of a prince over a republic, than that of a rustic over a herd of swine; as perchance the pleasures and delights of the one are greater than the pleasures and delights of the other. Therefore the loving and aspiring higher, brings with it greater glory and majesty, with more care, thought, and pain: I mean in this state, where the one opposite is always joined to the other, finding the greatest contrariety always in the same genus, and consequently about the same subject, although the opposites cannot be together. And thus proportionally in the love of the supernal Eros, as the Epicurean poet declares of vulgar and animal desire when he says:--

Fluctuat incertis erroribus ardor amantum,
Nec constat, quid primum oculis, manibusque fruantur:

Quod petiere, premunt arte, faciuntque dolorem
Corporis, et dentes inlidunt saepe labellis,
Osculaque adfigunt, quia non est pura voluptas,
Et stimuli subsunt, qui instigant laedere id ipsum,
Quodcunque est, rabies, unde illa haec germina surgant.
Sed leviter poenas frangit Venus inter amorem,
Blandaque refraenat morsus admixta voluptas;
Namque in eo spes est, unde est ardoris origo,
Restingui quoque posse ab eodem corpore flammam.

Behold, then, with what condiments the skill and art of nature works, so that one is wasted with the pleasure of that which destroys him, is happy in the midst of torment, and tormented in the midst of all the satisfactions. For nothing is produced absolutely from a homœogeneous (pacifico) principle, but all from opposite principles, through the victory and dominion of one part of the opposites, and there is no pleasure of generation on one side without the pain of corruption on the other: and where these things which are generated and corrupted are joined together and as it were compose the same subject, the feeling of delight and of sadness are found together; so that it comes to be called more easily delight than sadness, if it happens that this predominates, and solicits the senses with greater force.

III.

CES. Now let us take into consideration the following image which is that of a phœnix, which burns in the sun, and the smoke from which almost obscures the brightness of that by which it is set on fire, and here is the motto which says: Neque simile, nec par mar.

43. MAR.:

This phœnix set on fire by the bright sun,
Which slowly, slowly to extinction goes, The while she, girt with splendour burning lies;
Yields to her star antagonistic fief
Through that which towards the sky to Heaven ascends.
Black smoke, and sombre fog of murky hue
Concealing thus his radiance from our eyes,

And veiling that which makes her burn and shine.
And so my soul, illumined. and inflamed.
By radiance divine, would fain display
The brightness of her own effulgent thought;
The lofty concept of her song sends forth.
In words which do but hide the glorious light,
While I dissolve and melt and am destroyed
Ah me! this lowering cloud, this smoky fire of words
Abases that which it would elevate.

  CES. This fellow then says that as this phœnix act on fire by the sun and accustomed to light and flame comes to send upwards that smoke which obscures him who has rendered her so luminous, so he, the inflamed and illuminated enthusiast, through that which he does in praise of such an illustrious subject which has warmed his heart and which shines in his thought, comes rather to conceal it than to render it light for light, sending forth that smoke the effect of the flame, in which the substance of himself is resolved.

  MAR. I, without weighing and comparing the studies of that fellow, repeat what I said to you the other day, that praise is one of the greatest oblations that human affection can offer to an object. And leaving on one side the proposition of the Divine, tell me, who would have known of Achilles, Ulysses, and all the other Greek and Trojan chiefs? Who would have heard of all those great soldiers, the wise and the heroes of the earth, if they had not been placed amongst the stars and deified by the oblation of praise which has lighted the fire on the altar of the heart of illustrious poets and other singers, so that usually, the sacrificant, the victim and the sanctified deity, all mounted to the skies, through the hand and the vow of a worthy and lawful priest?

  CES. Well sayest thou "of a worthy and lawful priest," for the world is at present full of apostate ones, the which, as they are for the most part unworthy themselves, sing the praises of other unworthy ones, so that, asini asinos fricant. But Providence wills that these, instead of rising to the sky should go together to the shades of Orcus, so that naught is the glory of him who extols and of him who is extolled; for the one has woven a statue of straw, or carved the trunk of a tree, or cast a piece of chalk, and the other, the idol of shame and infamy, knows not that there is no need to wait for the keen tooth of the age and the scythe of Saturn in order to be put down, for through those self-same praises he gets buried alive then and there, while he is being praised, saluted, hailed, and presented. Just as it happened in a contrary way, so that much-praised Mœcenatus, who, if he had had no other glory than a soul inclined to protect and favour the Muses, for this alone merited, that the genius of so many illustrious poets should do him homage, and place him in the number of the most famous heroes who have trod this earth. His own studies and his own brightness made him prominent and grand, and not the being born of a royal race, and not the being grand secretary and councillor of Augustus. That, I say, which made him illustrious was the having made himself worthy to fulfil the promise of that poet who says:--

Fortunati ambo, si quid mea carmina possunt,
Nulla dies nunquam memori vos eximet sevo,
Dum domus Aeneae Capitoli immobile saxum
Accolet, imperiumque pater romanus habebit.

MAR. I remember what Seneca says in certain letters where he refers to the words of Epicurus to a friend, which are these: "If the love of glory is dear to thy breast, these letters of mine will make thee more famous and known than all those other things which thou honourest, by which thou art honoured, and of which thou mayest boast. The same might Homer have said if Achilles or Ulysses had presented themselves before him, or Eneas and his offspring before Virgil; as that moral philosopher well said; Domenea is more known through the letters of Epicurus, than all the magicians, satraps and royalties upon whom depended his title of Domenea and the memory of whom was lost in the depths of oblivion. Atticus does not survive because he was the son-in-law of Agrippa and ancestor of Tiberius, but through the epistles of Tully; Drusus, the ancestor of Cæsar, would not be found amongst the number of great names if Cicero had not inserted it. Many, many years may pass over our heads, and in all that time not many geniuses will keep their heads raised.

Now to return to the question of this enthusiast, who, seeing a phœnix set on fire by the sun, calls to mind his own cares, and laments that like the phœnix he sends, in exchange for the light and heat received, a sluggish smoke from the holocaust of his melted substance. Wherefore not only can we never discourse about things divine, but we cannot oven think of them without detracting from, rather than adding to the glory of them; so that the best thing to be done with regard to them is, that man, in the presence of other men, should rather praise himself for his earnestness and courage, than give praise to anything, as complete and perfected action; seeing that no such thing can be expected where there is progress towards the infinite, where unity and infinity are the same thing and cannot be followed by the other number, because there is no unity from another unity, nor is there number from another number and unity, because they are not the same absolute and infinite. Therefore was it well said by a theologian that as the fountain of light far exceeds not only our intellects, but also the divine, it is decorous that one should not discourse with words, but that with silence alone it should be magnified.

CES. Not, verily, with such silence as that of the brutes who are in the likeness and image of men, but of those whose silence is more exalted than all. the cries and noise and screams of those who may be heard.

IV.

MAR. Let us go on and see what the rest means.

CES. Say, if you have seen and considered it, what is the meaning of this fire in the form of a heart with four wings, two of which have eyes and the whole is girt with luminous rays and has round about it this question: Nitimur incassum?

MAR. I remember well, that it signifies the state of the mind, heart and spirit and eyes of the enthusiast, but read the sonnet!

44. Splendour divine, to which this mind aspires,
The intellect alone cannot unveil.
The heart, which those high thoughts would animate,

Makes not itself their lord; nor spirit, which
Should cease from pleasure for a space,
Can ever from those heights withdraw.
The eyes which should be closed at night in sleep,
Awake remain, open, and full of tears.
Ah me, my lights! where are the zeal and art
With which to tranquillize the afflicted sense?
Tell me my soul; what time and in what place
Shall I thy deep transcendent woo assuage?
And thou my heart, what solace can I bring
As compensation to thy heavy pain?
When, oh unquiet and perturbed mind,
Wilt thou the soul for debt and dole receive
With heart, with spirit and the sorrowing eyes?

The mind which aspires to the divine splendour flees from the society of the crowd and retires from the multitude of subjects, as much as from the community of studies, opinions and sentences; seeing that the peril of contracting vices and illusions is greater, according to the number of persons with whom one is allied. In the public shows, said the moral philosopher, by means of pleasure, vices are more easily engendered. If one aspires to the supreme splendour, let him retire as much as he can, from union and support, into himself (Di sorte che non sia simile a molti, per che son molti; e non sia nemico di molti per che son dissimili), so that he be not like unto many, because they are many; and be not adverse to many, because they are dissimilar; if it be possible, let him retain the one and the other; otherwise he will incline to that which seems to him best. Let him associate either with those whom he can make better or with those through whom he may be made better, through brightness which he may impart to those or that he may receive from them. Let him he content with one ideal rather than with the inept multitude. Nor will he hold that he has gained little, when he has become such an one who is wise unto himself, remembering what Democritus says: "Unus mihi pro populo est, et populus pro uno; and what Epicurus said to a companion of his studies, writing to him: "Haec tibi, non multis! Satis enim magnum alter alteri theatrum sumus."

The mind, then, which aspires high, leaves, for the first thing, caring about the crowd, considering that that divine light despises striving and is only to be found where there is intelligence, and yet not every intelligence, but that which is amongst the few, the chief. the first among the first, the principal one.

CES. How do you mean that the mind aspires high? For example, by looking at the stars? At the empyreal heaven above the ether?

MAR. Certainly not! but by plunging into the depths of the mind, for which there is no great need to open the eyes to the sky, to raise the hands, to direct the steps to the temple, nor sing to the ears of statues in order to be the better heard, but to come into the inner self believing that, God is near, present and within, more fully than man himself, being soul of souls, life of lives, essence of essences: for that which you see above or below, or round about, or however you please to say it, of the stars, are bodies, are created things, similar to this globe on which we are, and in which the divinity is present neither more nor less than he is in this globe of ours or in ourselves. This is how, then, one must begin to withdraw oneself from the multitude into oneself. One ought to arrive at such a point to despise and not to overestimate every labour, so that, the more the desires and the vices contend with each other inwardly and the vicious enemies dispute outwardly, so much the more should one breathe and rise, and with spirit, if possible, surmount this steep hill. Here there is no need for other arms and shield than the majesty of an unconquered soul and a tolerant spirit, which maintains the quality and meaning of that life which proceeds from science and is regulated by the art of considering attentively things low and high, divine and human, in the which consists that highest good, and in reference to this, a moral philosopher wrote to Lucillus that one must not linger between Scylla and Charybdis, penetrate the wilds of Candavia and the Apennines or lose oneself in the sandy plains, because the road is as sure and as blythe as Nature herself could make it. "It is not," says he, "gold and silver that makes one like God, because these are not treasure to Him; nor vestments, for God is naked; nor ostentation and fame, for He shows Himself to few, and perhaps not one knows Him, and certainly many, and more than many, have a bad opinion of Him. Not all the various conditions of things which we usually admire, for not those things of which we desire to have copies, make one rich, but the contempt for those things."

CES. Well. Bat tell me in what manner will this fellow tranquillize the senses, assuage the woes of the spirit, compensate the heart and give its just debts to the mind, so that with this aspiration of his he come not to say: "Nitimur incassum"?

MAR. He will be present in the body in such wise that the best part of himself will be absent from it, and will join himself by an indissoluble sacrament to divine things, in such a way that he will not feel either love or hatred of things mortal. Considering himself as master, and that he ought not to be servant and slave to his body, which he would regard only as the prison which holds his liberty in confinement, the glue which smears his wings, chains which bind fast his hands, stocks which fix his feet, veil which hides his view. Let him not be servant, captive, ensnared, chained, idle, stolid and blind, for the body which he himself abandons cannot tyrannize over him, so that thus, the spirit in a certain degree comes before him as the corporeal world, and matter is subject to the divinity and to nature. Thus will he become strong against fortune, magnanimous towards injuries, intrepid towards poverty, disease and persecution.

CES. Well is the heroic enthusiast instructed!

V.

CES. Close by is to be seen that which follows. See the wheel of time, which moves round its own centre, and there is the legend. "Manens moveor." What do you mean by that?

MAR. This means that movement is circular where motion concurs with rest, seeing that in orbicular motion upon its own axis and about its own centre is understood rest and stability according to right movement, or, rest of the whole and movement of the parts; and from the parts which move in a circle is understood two different kinds of motion, inasmuch as some parts rise to the summit and others from the summit descend to the base successively; others reach the medium differences, and others the extremes of high and low. And all this seems to me suitably expressed in the following:

45. That which keeps my heart both open and, concealed,
Beauty imprints and honesty dispels;
Zeal holds me fast; all other care comes to me
By that same path whence all care to the soul doth come:
Seek I myself from pain to disengage,
Hope sustains me then whose scourges, tires;--(altrui rigor mi lassa)
Love doth exalt and reverence abase me
What time I yearn towards the highest good.
High thoughts, holy desires, and mina intent
Upon the labours and the cunning of the heart
Towards the immense divine immortal object,
So do, that I be joined, united, fed,
That I lament no more; that reason, sense, attend,
Discourse and penetrate to other things.

SO that the continual movement of one part supposes and carries with it the movement of the whole, in such a way that the attraction of the posterior parts is consequent upon the repulsion of the anterior parts; thus the movement of the superior parts results of necessity from that of the inferior, and from the raising of one opposite power, follows the depression of the other opposite. Therefore the heart, which signifies all the affections generally, comes to be concealed and open, held by zeal, raised by magnificent thoughts, sustained by hope, weakened by fear, and in this state and condition will it ever be seen and found.

VI.

CES. That is all well. Let us come to that which follows. I see a ship floating on the waves; its ropes are attached to the shore and there is the legend. Fluctuat in portu. Deliberate about the signification of this, and when you are decided about it, explain.

MAR. Both the legend and the figure have a certain connexion with the present legend and figure, m may be easily understood, if one considers it a little. But let us read the sonnet.

46. If I by gods, by heroes and by men
Be re-assured, so that I not despair,
Nor fear, pain, nor the impediments
Of death of body, joy and happiness,
Yet must I learn to suffer and to feel.
And that I may my pathways clearly see,
Let doubts arise, and dolour, and the woe
Of vanished hopes, of joy and all delight.
But if he should behold, should grant, and should attend
My thoughts, my wishes, and my reasoning,
Who makes them so uncertain, hot, and vague,
Such dear conceits, such acts and speech,
Will not be given nor done to him, who stays
From birth, through life, to death in sheltered home.

Non dà, non fa, non ha qualunque stassi
Do l'orto, vita e morte a le magioni.

From what we have considered and said in the preceding discourses one is able to understand these sentiments, especially where it is shown that the sense of low things is diminished and annulled whenever the superior powers are strongly intent upon a more elevated and heroic object. The power of contemplation is so great, as is noted by Jamblichus, that it happens sometimes, not only that the soul ceases from inferior acts, but that it leaves the body entirely. The which I will not understand otherwise than in such various ways as are explained in the book of thirty seals, wherein are produced so many methods of contraction, of which some infamously, others heroically operate, that one learns not to fear death, suffers not pain of body, feels not the hindrances of pleasures: wherefore the hope, the joy, and the delight of the superior spirit are of so intense a kind that they extinguish all those passions which may have their origin in doubt, in pain and all kinds of sadness.

CES. But what is that, of which he requests that it consider those thoughts which it has rendered so uncertain, fulfil those desires which it has made so ardent, and listen to those discourses which it has rendered so vague?

MAR. He means the Object, which he beholds when it makes itself present; for to see the Divine is to be seen by it, as to see the sun concurs, with the being seen of the sun. Equally, to be heard by the Divine, is precisely to listen to it, and to be favoured by it, is the same as to offer to it; for from the one immoveable and the same, proceed thoughts uncertain and certain, desires ardent and appeased, and reasonings valid and vain, according as the man worthily or unworthily puts them before himself, with the intellect, the affections and actions. As that same pilot may be said to be the cause of the sinking or of the safety of the ship, according as he is present in it or absent from it; with this difference, that the pilot through his defectiveness or his efficiency ruins or saves the ship; but the Divine potency which is all in all does not proffer or withhold except through assimilation or rejection by oneself.

VII.

MAR. It seems to me that the following figure is closely connected and linked with the above; there are two stars in the form of two radiant eyes, with the legend: Mors et vita.

CES. Read the sonnet!

MAR. I will do so:

47. Writ by the hand of Love may each behold
Upon my face the story of my woes.
But thou, so that thy pride no curb may know,
And I, unhappy one, eternally might rest,
Thou dost torment, by hiding from my view
Those lovely lights beneath the beauteous lids.
Therefore the troubled sky's no more serene,
Nor hostile baleful shadows fall away.
By thine own beauty, by this love of mine
(So great that e'en with this it may compare),
Render thyself, oh Goddess, unto pity!
Prolong no more this all-unmeasured woe,
Ill-timed reward for such a love as this.
Let not such rigour with such splendour mate

If it import thee that I live!
Open, oh lady, the portals of thine eyes,
And look on me if thou wouldst give me death!

Here, the face upon which the story of his woes appears is the soul, in so far as it is open to receive those superior gifts, for the which it has a potential aptitude, without the fulness of perfection and act which waits for the dew of heaven. Thus was it well said. Anima mea sicut terra siue aqua tibi; and again: Os meum operui; and again: Spiritum, quia mandata tua desiderabam. Then, "pride which knows no curb" is said in metaphor and similitude, as God is sometimes said to be jealous, angry, or that He sleeps, and that signifies the difficulty with which He grants so much even as to show his shoulders, which is the making himself known by means of posterior things and effects. So the lights are covered with the eyelids, the troubled sky of the human mind does not clear itself by the removal of the metaphors and enigmas. Besides which, because he does not believe that all which is not, could not be, he prays the divine light, that by its beauty, which ought not to be entirely concealed, at least according to the capacity of whoever beholds it, and by his love, which, perchance, is equal to so much beauty (equal, he means, of the beauty, in so far as he can comprehend it) that it surrender itself to pity, that is, that it should do as those who are compassionate, and who from being capricious and gloomy become gracious and affable and that it prolong not the evil which results from that privation, and not allow that its splendour, for which it is so much desired, should appear greater than that love by means of which it communicates itself, seeing that in it all the perfections are not only equal but are also the same. In fine, he begs that it will no further sadden by privation, for it can kill with the glance of its eyes and can also with those same give him life.

CES. Does he mean that death of lovers, which comes from intense joy, called by the Kabalists, mors osculi, which same is eternal life, which a man may anticipate in this life and enjoy in eternity?

MAR. He does.

VIII.

MAR. It is time to proceed to the consideration of the following design, similar to those previously brought forward, and with which it has a certain affinity. There is an eagle, which with two wings cleaves the sky; but I do not know how much and in what manner it comes to be retarded by the weight of a stone which is tied to its leg. There is the legend: Scinditur incertum. It is certain that it signifies the multitude, number and character (volgo) of the powers of the soul, to exemplify which, that verse is taken: Scinditur incertum studia in contraria vulgus. The whole of which character (volgo) in general is divided into two factions; although subordinate to these, others are not wanting, of which some appeal to the high intelligence and splendour of rectitude, while others incite and force in a certain manner to the low, to the uncleanness of voluptuousness and compliance with natural desires. Therefore says the sonnet:

48. I would do well--to me 'tis not allowed.
With me my sun is not, although I be with him,
For being with him, I'm no more with myself:
The farther from myself-the nearer unto him;
The nearer unto him, the farther from myself.
Once to enjoy, doth cost me many tears,
And seeking happiness, I meet with woo.
For that I look aloft, so blind am I.
That I may gain my love, I lose myself.
Through bitter joy, and through sweet pain,
Weighted with lead, I rise towards the sky.
Necessity withholds, goodness conducts me on,
Fate sinks me down, and counsel raises me,
Desire spurs me, fear keeps me in cheek.
Care kindles and the peril backward draws.
Ten me, what power or what subterfuge
Can give me peace and bring me from this strife,
If one repels, the other draws me on.

The ascension goes on in the soul through the power and appulsion in the wings, which are the intellect, or intellectual will upon which she naturally depends and through which she fixes her gaze toward God, as to the highest good, and primal truth, as to absolute goodness and beauty. Thus everything has an impetus towards its beginning retrogressively, and progressively towards its end and perfection, as Empedocles well said, and from which sentence I think may be inferred that which the Nolan said in this octave:

The sun must turn and reach his starting-point,
Each wandering light must go towards its source,
That which is earth to earth itself reverts,
The rivers from the sea to sea return,
And thither, whence desires have life and grow
Must they aspire as to revered divinity,
So every thought born of my lady fair
Comes back perforce to her, my goddess dear.

The intellectual power is never at rest, it is never satisfied with any comprehended truth, but ever proceeds on and on towards that truth which is not comprehended. So also the will which follows the apprehension, we see that it is never satisfied with anything finite. In consequence of this, the essence of the soul is always referred to the source of its substance and entity. Then as to the natural powers, by means of which it is turned to the protection and government of matter, to which it allies itself, and by appulsion benefits and communicates of its perfection to inferior things, through the likeness which it has to the Divine, which in its benignity communicates itself or produces infinitely, *i.e.* imparts existence to the universal infinite and to the innumerable worlds in it, or, finitely, produces this universe alone, subject to our eyes and our common reason. Thus then in the one sole essence of the soul are found these two kinds of powers, and as they are used for one's own good and for the good of others, it follows that they are depicted with a pair of wings, by means of which it is potent towards the object of the primal and immaterial potencies, and with a heavy stone, through which it is active and efficacious towards the objects of the secondary and material potencies. Whence it follows that the entire affection of the enthusiast is bifold, divided, harassed, and placed in a position to incline itself more easily downwards than to force itself upwards: seeing that the soul finds itself in a low and hostile country, and reaches the far-off region of its more natural home where its powers are the weakest.

CES. Do you think that this difficulty can be overcome?

MAR. Perfectly well; but the beginning is most difficult, and according as we make more and more fruitful progress in contemplation we arrive at a greater and greater facility. As happens to whoever flys up high, the more he rises above the earth the more air he has beneath to uphold him, and consequently the less he is affected by gravitation; he may even rise so high that he cannot, without the labour of cleaving the air, return downwards, although one might imagine it were more easy to cleave the air downwards towards the earth than to rise on high towards the stars.

CES. So that with progress of this kind a greater and greater facility is acquired for mounting on high?

MAR. So it is; therefore well said Tansillo:--

"The more I feel the air beneath my feet
So much the more towards the wind I bend
My swiftest pinions
And spurn the world and up towards Heaven I go."

As every part of bodies and of their elements, the nearer they come to their natural place, the greater the impetus and force with which they move, until at last, whether they will or not, they must prevail. That which we see then in the parts of bodies and in the bodies themselves we ought also to allow of intellectual things towards their proper objects, as their proper places, countries, and ends. Whence you may easily comprehend the entire significance of the figure, the legend, and the verses.

CES. So much so that whatsoever you might add thereto would appear to me superfluous.

IX.

CES. Let us see what is here represented by those two radiating arrows upon a target around, which is written: Vicit instans.

MAR. The continual struggle in the soul of the enthusiast, the which, in consequence of the long familiarity which it had with matter was hard and incapable of being penetrated by the rays of the splendour of the Divine intelligence and the species of the Divine goodness; during which time, he says that the heart was enamelled with diamond, that is, the affection was hard and not capable of being heated and penetrated, and it rejected the blows of love which assailed it on innumerable sides. That is, it did not feel itself wounded by those wounds of eternal life of which the Psalmist speaks when he says: Vulnerasti cor meum, o dilecta, vulnerasti cor meum. The which wounds are not from iron or other material through the vigour and strength of nerves, but are darts of Diana, or of Phœbus, that is, either from the goddess of the deserts--of contemplation of truth, that is, from Diana, who is the order of the second intelligences, which transfer the splendour received from the first and communicate, it to the others. who are deprived of a more open vision; or else from the principal god Apollo, who, with his own, and not a borrowed splendour, sends his darts, that is, his rays, so many and from such innumerable points, which are all the species of things, which are indications of Divine goodness, intelligence, beauty, and wisdom. according to the, various degrees, from the simple comprehension, to the becoming heroic enthusiasts; because the adamantine subject does not reflect from its surface, the impression of the light, but, destroyed and overcome by the heat and light, it becomes in substance luminous--all light--so that it is penetrated within the affection and conception. This is not immediately, at the beginning of generation, when the soul comes forth fresh from the intoxication of Lethe, and drenched with the waves of forgetfulness and confusion, so that the spirit comes into captivity to the body, and is put into the condition of growth; but little by little, it goes on digesting, so as to become fitted for the action of the sensitive faculty, until, through the rational and discursive faculty, it comes to a purer intellectual one, so that it can present itself to the mind, without feeling itself be. fogged by the exhalations of that humour, which, through the exercise of contemplation, has been saved from putrefaction in the stomach and is duly digested. In this state, the present enthusiast shows himself to have remained thirty years, during which time he had not reached that purity of conception which would make him a suitable habitation for the wandering species, which offering themselves to all, equally, knock, ever at the door of the intelligence. At last, Love, who in various ways and at different times had assaulted him as it were in vain--as the light and heat of the sun are said to be useless to those who are in the opaque depths and bowels of the earth--having located itself in those sacred lights, that is having shown forth the Divine Beauty through two intelligible species the which bound his intellect through the reasoning of Truth and warmed his affections through the reasoning of Goodness; while the material and sensitive desires became superseded, which aforetime used, as it were, to triumph, remaining intact, notwithstanding the excellence of the soul. Because those lights which made present the illuminating, acting intellect and sun of intelligence found easy ingress through his eyes; that of Truth (the intellect of Truth?) through the door of the intellectual faculty; that of Goodness(intellect of Goodness?) through the door of the appetitive faculty, to the heart, that is, the substance of the general affection. This was that double ray, which came as from the hand of an irate warrior, who showed himself, now, as ready and as bold, as; aforetime he had appeared weak and negligent.

Then, when he first felt warmed and illuminated in his conception, was that victorious point and moment of which it is said: Vicit instans.

Thus you can understand the sense of the following figure, legend and sonnet, which says:--

49. I fought with all my strength 'gainst Love Divine
When he assailed with blows from every side
This cold, enamelled, adamantine heart,
Whence my desires defeated his intent.
At last, one day, 'twas as the heavens had willed.
Encamped I found him in those holy lights
Which, through mine own alone, of all the rest
An easy entrance to my heart could find.
'Twas then upon me fell that double bolt,
Flung as from hand of irate warrior
Who had for thirty years besieged in vain.

He marked that place and strongly there he held,
Planted the trophy there, and evermore
He holds my fleet wings in restrainment.
Meanwhile since then with more solemnity of preparation
The anger and the ire of my sweet enemy
Cease not to wound my heart.

Rare moment was that; the end of the beginning and perfection of victory; rare were those two species which amongst all others found easy entrance, seeing that they contain in themselves the efficacy and the virtue of all the others; for what higher and more excellent form can present itself than that of the beauty, goodness and truth, which are the source of every other truth, beauty, and goodness? "He marked that place"--that is, took possession of the affections, noted them, and impressed upon them his own character; "and strongly there he held;" he confirmed and established them and sanctified them so that he can never again lose them; for it is not possible that one should turn to love any other thing when once he has conceived in his mind the Divine Beauty, and it is as impossible that he can do other than love it, as it is impossible that his desires should fall otherwise than towards good, or species of good. Therefore his inclination is in the highest degree towards the primal good. So again, the wings, which used to be so fleet to go downwards with the weight of matter, are kept in restrainment, and the sweet angers which are the efficacious assaults of the gracious enemy, who has been for so long time kept back, and excluded, a stranger and a pilgrim, never cease to wound, soliciting the affections and awakening thought. Bat now, the sole and entire possessor and disposer of the soul, for she neither wills nor wishes to will other, nor is she pleased, nor will she that any other please her, whence he often says:--

Dolci ire, guerra dolce, dolci dardi,
Dolci mie piaghe, miei dolci dolori!

X.

CES. It would seem that we have nothing more to consider upon this proposition. Let us see now, how this quiver and bow of Bros display the sparks around, and the knot of the string, which hangs, down with the legend, which is: Subito, clam.

MAR. Well do I remember having seen it expressed in the sonnet. But let us read it first.

50. Eager to find the much desired food,
The eagle towards the sky spreads out his wings
And wafts of his approach both bird and beast,
The third flight bringing him upon the prey.
And the fierce lion roaring from his lair
Spreads horror all around and mortal fear;
And all wild beasts, admonished and forewarned,
Fly to the caves and cheat his cruel jaw.
The whale, ere he the dumb Protean herd
Hungry pursues, sends forth his nuncio,
From caves of Thetys spouts his water forth.
Lions and eagles of the earth and sky,
And whales, lords of the seas, come not with treachery,
But the assaults of Love come stealing secretly.

The animal kingdom is divided into three, and is composed of various elements: the earth, the water, the air, and there are three species--beasts, fishes, and birds. Into three kinds are the principles of nature settled and defined, in the air the eagle, on earth the lion, in the water the whale; of the which, each one, as it displays more strength and. command over the others, makes a show of magnanimous action. or apparently magnanimous. Therefore it is observed, that the lion, before he starts on the hunt trumpets forth his roar, which resounds through the whole forest, like to the poetic description of the fury-hunter.

At saeva e speculis tempus dea nacta, nocendi,
Ardua tecta petit, stabuli et de culmine summo
Pastorale canit signum, cornuque recurvo
Tartaream intendit vocem, qua protinus omne
Contremuit nemus, et silvae intonuere profundae.

The eagle again, before he proceeds to his venery, first rises straight from the nest in a perpendicular line upwards, and generally speaking at the third time he swoops from above with greater impetus and swiftness than if he were flying in a direct line, so that at the time when be is gaining the greatest velocity of flight, he is able also to speculate upon his success with the prey, and after three inspections he knows whether be will succeed or fail.

CES. Can one imagine why, if at the first his prey presents itself before his eyes, he does not instantly pounce upon it?

MAR. No; unless it be to see whether anything better, or more easily taken, comes to sight, At the, same time I do not believe that this is always so, but most often. it is. But to return. Of the whale it is manifest that, being such a huge animal, he cannot divide the waters without making his presence known through the repulsion of the waves, besides which there are several species of this fish, that when they move or breathe, spout forth a windy tempest of water. Thus from these three, principal species of animals, the inferior kinds have warning to enable them to get away, so that they do not conduct themselves as deceivers and traitors. But Love, who is stronger and greater and who has

supreme dominion in heaven, on earth, and in the seas, and who in comparison ought perhaps to show greater magnanimity, as he also has more power, does nothing of the kind, but assaults and wounds suddenly and swiftly.

Labitur totas furor in medullas,
Igne furtivo populante venas,
Nec habet latum data plaga frontem;
Sed vorat tectas penitas medullas,
Virginum ignoto ferit igne pectus.

As you perceive, the tragic poet calls him a furtive fire, an unknown flame. Solomon calls it furtive waters. Samuel named it the whisper of a gentle wind. The which three significations show with what sweetness, gentleness, and astuteness, in seas, on earth, in sky, does this fellow come and tyrannize over the whole universe.

CES. There is no vaster empire, no worse tyranny, no better dominion, no more necessary magistracy, nothing more sweet and dear, no food to be found more hard and bitter, no deity more violent, no god more pleasing, no agent more treacherous and false, no author more regal and faithful, and, in fine, it seems to me that Love is all and does all, of him all may be said, and all may refer itself to him.

MAR. You say well. Love then, as he who works chiefly through the sight, which is the most spiritual of all the senses, and which reaches swiftly the known ends of the earth, and without stretch of time takes in the whole horizon of the visible, comes to be quick, furtive, sudden and instantaneous. Besides which, we must remember what the ancients say, that Love precedes all the other gods, and therefore it is no use to imagine that Saturn shows him the way except by following him. Now must we find out, whether Love appears and makes himself known externally, whether his home is the soul itself, his bed the heart itself, and whether he consists of the same composition as our own substance, the same impulse as our own powers. Finally everything naturally desires the beautiful and the good, and therefore it is useless to argue and discuss, because the affection informs and confirms itself, and in one instant desire joins itself to the desirable, as the sight to the visible.

XI.

CES. Let us see here, what is the meaning of that burning arrow, around which is the legend: Cui nova plaga loco? Explain what part does this seek to wound?

MAR. Read the sonnet which says:--
That all the ears of corn that may be reaped
In burning Apuleia, or sunbrowned Lybia,
With all that they unto the winds entrust,
Or that the rays from the great planet sent,
Should number those sad pains of my glad soul,
Which she from those two burning stars receives
With mournful joy in sweetest agony,
Forbid me Sense and Reason to believe.
What would'st thou more, sweet foe?
What wish is that which moves thee still to hurt,
Since this my heart of but one wound is made?
So that there lies no part that now may be
By thee or others printed, stabbed, or pierced,

Turn thee aside, turn otherwhere thy bow,
For thou dost waste thy powers, oh beauteous god!
In slaying him who lies already dead. The meaning of all this is metaphorical, like the rest, and may be understood in the same sense as that. Here the number of darts which have wounded and do wound the heart, signify the innumerable individuals and species of things, in which shine the splendour of Divine Beauty, according to their degrees and whence the affection for the good, well proposed and well apprehended warms us. The which throng the causes of potentiality and actuality, of possibility and of effect, crucify and console, give the sense of sweetness and also make the bitter to be felt. But where the entire affection is all turned toward God that is towards the Idea of Ideas, from the light of intelligible things, the mind becomes exalted to the super-essential unity, and.. all love, all one, it feels itself no longer solicited by various objects, which distract it, but is one sole wound, in the which the whole affection concurs and which comes to be one and. the same affection. Then there is no love or desire of any particular thing, that can urge, nor even present itself before the will; for there is nothing more straight than the straight, nothing more beautiful than beauty, nothing better than goodness, nothing can be found larger than size, nor anything lighter than that light which with its presence darkens and obliterates all lights.

CES. To the perfect, if it be perfect, there is nothing that can be added; therefore the will is not capable of any other desire, when that which is of the perfect is present with it, highest and best. Therefore I understand the conclusion where be says to Love, "Turn otherwhere thy bow," and wherefore should he try to kill him who is already dead, that is, he, who has no more life nor sense about other things, so that he cannot be stabbed or pierced or become exposed to other species. And this lame proceeds from him, who having tasted of the highest unity, desires to be in all things severed and withdrawn from the multitude.

MAR. You understand quite well.

XII.

CES. Now here is a boy in a boat, which little by little is being submerged in the tempestuous waves, and he, languid and tired, has abandoned the oars; around it the legend "Fronti nulla fides." There is no doubt that this signifies that he was induced, by the serene aspect of the waters, to venture on the treacherous sea, which having suddenly become troubled, the boy, in mortal fear, and in his impotence to still the tempest, has lost his head, his hope, and the power of his arm. But let us see the rest:--

52. Oh, gentle boy, that from the shore didst loose
The baby bark, and to the slender oar
Didst set thy unskilled hand; lured by the sea!
Late hast thou seen the evil of thy plight.
See there the traitor rolls his fatal waves,
The prow of thy frail bark, now sinks, now mounts.
The soul borne down with anxious cares
Prevaileth not against the swollen floods.
Thy oars thou yieldst to thy fierce enemy,
Waiting for death with calm collected thought,
With eyelids closed, lest thou shouldst see him come.
If thee no friendly aid should quickly reach
Thou surely must the full result soon feel,
Of thy inquisitive temerity.
My cruel fate is like unto thine own,
For I too, lured, enticed by Love, must feel,
The rigour keen of this most treacherous one.

In what manner and why Love is a traitor and deceiver we have just seen; but as I see the following without figure or legend, I believe that it must have connection with the above. Therefore let us go on and read it.

53. Methought to leave the shelter of my port,
And from maturer studies rest awhile.
When, looking round me to enjoy my ease,
Sudden I saw those unrelenting fates.
These have inflamed me with so ardent fires.
Vainly I strive some safer shores to reach,
Vainly from pitying hands invoke some aid,

And swift deliverance from my enemies.
Weary and hoarse I yield me, impotent,
And seek no more to elude my destiny,
Or make endeavour to escape my death:
Let every other life to me be null,
And let not the extremest torment fail,
Which my hard fate for me prescribed.
Type of my own deep ills,
Is that which thou for pastime didst entrust
To hostile breast. Oh, careless boy.

Here I would not pretend to understand or determine all that the enthusiast means. Yet there is well expressed the strange condition of a soul cast down by the knowledge of the difficulty of the operation, the amount of the labour, the vastness of the work on one side, and on the other the ignorance, want of knowledge of the way, weakness of nerves and peril of death. He has no knowledge suitable to the business, he does not know where and how to turn, no place of flight or refuge presents itself; and he sees that, from every side, the waves threaten, with frightful, fatal impetus. Ignoranti portum, nullus suus ventas est. Behold him, who has committed himself indeed to fortuitous things, and has brought upon himself trouble, prison, rain, and drowning. See how fortune deludes us, and that which we put carefully into her hands, she either breaks or lets it fall from her hands, or causes it to be removed by the violence of another, or suffocates and poisons, or taints with suspicion, fear, and jealousy to the great hurt and ruin of the possessor. Fortunae au ulla putatis dona carcere dolis? For strength which cannot give proof of itself is dissipated; magnanimity, which cannot prevail, is naught, and vain is study without results; he sees the effects of the fear of evil, which is worse than evil itself. Peior est morte timor ipse mortis. He already suffers, through fear, that which he fears to suffer, terror in the limbs, imbecility in the nerves, tremors in the body, anxiety of the spirit, and that which has not yet appeared becomes present to him, and is certainly worse than whatsoever may happen. What can be more stupid than to be in pain about future, things and absent ones which at present are not felt?

Cu. These considerations are on the surface and belong to the external of the figure. But the proposition of the heroic enthusiast, I think, deals with the imbecility of human nature (ingegno) which, intent on the Divine undertaking, finds itself all at once engulphed in the abyss of incomprehensible excellence, and the sense and the imagination become confused and absorbed, and not knowing how to pass on, nor to go back, nor where to turn, vanishes and loses itself as a drop of water vanishes in the sea, or as a small spirit, becomes attenuated, losing its own substance in the space and immensity of the atmosphere.

MAR. Well. But let us go towards our chamber and. talk as we go, for it is night.

Second Dialogue

MARICONDO. Here you see a flaming yoke enveloped in knots round which is written: Levius aura; which means that Divine love does not weigh down, nor carry his servant captive and enslaved to the lowest depths, but raises him, supports him and magnifies him above all liberty whatsoever.

CES. Prithee, let us read the sonnet, so that we may consider the sense of it in due order with propriety and brevity.

MAR. It says thus:--

54. She who my mind to other love did move,
To whom all others vile and vain appear,
In whom alone is sovereign beauty seen,
And excellence Divine is manifest.
She from the forest coming, I beheld,
Huntress of myself, beloved Artemis,
'Midst beauteous nymphs, with air of nascent bells.
Then said I unto Love: See, I am hers.
And he to me: Oh, happy lover thou!
Delectable companion of thy fate!
That she alone of all the numberless,
That hold within their bosom life and death,
Who most with virtues high the world adorns,
Thou didst obtain, through will and destiny,
Within the Court of Love.
So happy thou in thy captivity
Thou enviest not the liberty of man or God.

See how contented he is under that yoke, that marriage which has joined him to her whom be saw issuing from the forest, from the desert, from the woods, that is, from parts removed from the crowd, and from the conversation of the vulgar who have but small enlightenment. Diana, the splendour of the intelligible species, and huntress; because with her beauty and grace she first wounded him, and then bound him and holds him in her power, more contented than otherwise he could possibly have been. He speaks of her "amidst beauteous nymphs," that is, the multitude of other species, forms and ideas, and "air of bells," that is the genius and the spirit which displayed itself at Nola, which lies on the plain of the Campanian horizon. He acknowledges her, and she, more than any other, is praised by Love, who considers him so fortunate, because amongst all those present or absent to, mortal eyes, she does more highly adorn the world, and makes man glorious and beautiful. Hence he says that his mind is raised towards the highest love, and that it learns to consider "every other goddess," that is, the care or observation of every other kind, as vile and vain. Now, in saying that she has roused his mind to high love, he takes occasion to magnify the heart through the thoughts, desires and works, as much as possible, and (to say) that we ought not to be entertained with low things which are beneath our faculties, as happens to those who, through avarice or through negligence, or indolence, become in this brief life attached to unworthy things.

CES. There must be artisans, mechanics, agriculturists, servants, trotters, ignoble, low, poor, pedants and such like, for otherwise there could not be philosophers, meditators, cultivators of souls, masters, captains, nobles, illustrious ones, rich, wise, and the rest who may be heroes like to gods. Now why should we force ourselves to corrupt the state of mature which has separated the universe into things major and minor, superior and inferior, illustrious and obscure, worthy and unworthy, not only outside ourselves but also inside in the substance of us, even to that part of us which is said to be immaterial?

So of the intelligences: some are low, others are pre-eminent, some serve and some obey, some command and govern. I believe, however, that this ought not to be brought forward as an example, so that subjects wishing to be superiors, and the ignoble to equal the noble, the order of things would become perverted and confounded, so that a sort of neutrality would supervene, and a brutal equality, such as is found in certain deserts and uncultured republics. Do you not see what damage has been done to science through this: *i.e.* pedants wishing to be philosophers; to treat of natural things, and mix themselves with and decide about things Divine r Who does not see how much evil has happened, and does happen, through the mind having been moved through similar facts to exalted affections? Who. is there, of good sense, who cannot see what a fine. thing Aristotle made of it, when, being a master of belles lettres at Alexandria, he set him self to oppose. and make war against the Pythagorean doctrine, and that of natural philosophy; seeking by means of his logical ratiocination to propose definitions and notions, certain fifth entities and other abortive portions of fantastical cogitations, as principles and substance of things, more anxious about the esteem of the vulgar stupid crowd, which is influenced and governed by sophisms and appearances which are found in the superficies of things rather than by the Truth, which is occult and hidden in the substance of them, and is the substance itself of them? He roused his mind, not to make himself a mediator, but judge and censor of things which he had never studied. nor well understood. Thus in our day, that little which Aristotle can bring, is peculiar for its inventive reasoning, its suggestiveness, its metaphysics, and is useful for other pedants, who work with the same "Sursum corda." who institute new dialectics and modes of forming the reason (judgment?) which are as much viler than those of Aristotle, as may be the philosophy of Aristotle is incomparably viler than that of the ancients. And it has been caused by this, that certain grammarians having grown old in the birching of children, and in anatomizing phrases and words, have sought to rouse the mind to the formation of new logic and metaphysics, judging and sentencing those which they had never studied nor understood: as also these by the approbation of the ignorant multitude, with whose mind they have most affinity, can easily demolish the humanities and ratiocination of Aristotle, as the latter was the executioner of the Divine philosophies of others. See, then, what it comes to, if all should aspire to the sacred splendour, and yet are occupied about things low and vain.

MAR.

Ride, si sapis, o puella, ride,
Pelignus, puto, dixerat poeta;
Sed non dixerat omnibus puellis;
Et si dixerat omnibus puellis,
Non dixit tibi. Ta puella, non es.

Thus the "Sursum corda" is not the measure for all; but for those that have wings. We see that pedantry has never been held in such esteem for the government of the world as in our times, and it offers as many paths of the true intelligible species and objects of infallible and sole truth as there are individual pedants. Therefore in this present time it is proper that noble spirits equipped with truth and enlightened with the Divine intelligence, should arm themselves against dense ignorance by climbing up to the high rock and tower of contemplation.

To them it is seemly that they hold every other object as vile and vain. Nor should these spend their time in light and vain things; for time flies with infinite velocity; the present rushes by with the same swiftness with which the future draws near. That which we have lived is nothing; that which we live is a point; that which we have to live is not yet a point, but may be a point which, together, shall be and shall have been. And with all this we crowd our memories with genealogies: this one is intent upon the deciphering of writings, that other is occupied in multiplying childish sophisms, and we shall see, for example, a volume full of: Cor est fons vitae. Nix est alba, ergo cornix est fons vitae alba, and one prattles about the noun; was it first, or the verb; the other, whether the sea was first or the springs; again, another tries to revive obsolete vocabularies which, because they were once used and approved by some old writer, must now be exalted to the stars. Yet another takes his stand upon the false or the true orthography, and so on, with various similar nonsense only worthy of contempt. They fast, they become thin and emaciated, they scourge the skin, and lengthen the beard, they rot, and in these things they place the anchor of their highest good. They despise fortune, and put up these as shield and refuge against the strokes of fate. With such-like most vile thoughts they think to mount to the stars, to be equal to gods, and to understand the good and the beautiful which philosophy promises.

CES. A grand thing, indeed, that time, which does not suffice for necessary things, however carefully we use it, should come to be chiefly consumed about superfluous things, and things vile and shameful.

Is it not rather a thing to laugh at than to praise in Archimedes, that at the time when the city was in confusion, everything in ruins, fire broken out in his room, enemies there at his back who had it in their power to make him lose his brain, his life, his art; that he, meanwhile, having abandoned all desire or intention of saving his life, lost it while he was inquiring, perhaps, into the proportion of the curve to the straight line, of the diameter to the circle, or other similar mathesis, as suitable for youth, as it were unsuitable for one who, being old, should. be intent upon things more worthy of being put as the end of human desires?

MAR. In connection with this I like what you said just now, that there must be all sorts of persons in the world, and that the number of the imperfect, the ugly, the poor, the unworthy and the villanous, should be the greater, and, in short, it ought not to be otherwise than as it is. The long life of Archimedes, of Euclid, of Priscian, of Donato, and others, who were found up to their death occupied with numbers, lines, diction, concordances, writings, dialectics, syllogisms, forms, methods, systems of science, organs, and other preambles, is ordained for the service of youth, so that they may learn to receive the fruits of the mature age of those (sages) and be full of the same, even in their green age, so that when they are older they may be fit and ready to arrive without hindrance to higher things.

CES. I am not wrong in the proposition I moved just now when I spoke of those who make it their study to appropriate to themselves the place and the fame of the ancients with new works which are neither better nor worse than those already existing, and spend their life in considering how to turn wheat into tares, and find the work of their life in the elaboration of those studies which are suited for children and are generally profitable to no one, not even to themselves.

MAR. But enough has been said about those who neither can nor dare to have their mind roused to highest love. Let us now come to the consideration of the voluntary captivity and of the pleasant yoke under the dominion of the said Diana; that yoke, I say, without which, the soul is impotent to rise to that height from which it fell, and which renders it light and agile, while the noose renders it more active and disengaged.

CES. Speak on then!

MAR. To begin, to continue, and to conclude in order; I consider that all which lives must feed itself and nourish itself in a manner suitable to the way in which it lives. Therefore, nothing squares with the intellectual nature but the intellectual, as with the body nothing but the corporeal; seeing that nourishment is taken for no other reason, but that it should go to the substance of him who is to be nourished. As then the body does not transmute into spirit, nor the spirit into body,-- for every transmutation takes place, when matter, which was in one form, comes to be in another, --so the spirit and the body are not the same matter; in that that, which was subject to one should come to be subject to the other.

CES. Surely, if the soul should be nourished with body, it would carry itself better there, where the fecundity of the material is, (as Jamblichus argues); so that when a large fat body presents itself, we should imagine that it were the habitation of a strong soul, firm, ready and heroic, and we should say; Oh, fat soul, oh, fecund spirit, oh, fine nature, oh, divine intelligence, ob, clear mind, oh, blessed repast, fit to spread before lions, or verily for a banquet for dogs. On the other hand, an old man shrivelled, weak, of failing strength, would be held to be of little savour and of small account. But go on.

MAR. Now, it must be said that the outcome of the mind is that alone which is always by it desired, sought for, and embraced, and that which is more enjoyed than anything else, with which it is filled, comforted and becomes better,--that is Truth, towards which, in all times, in every state, and in whatsoever condition man finds himself, he always aspires, and for the which he despises every fatigue, attempt, every study, makes no account of the body, and hates this life. Therefore Truth is an incorporeal thing, and neither physics, metaphysics, nor mathematician be found in the body, because we see that the eternal human essence is not in individuals, who are born and die. It (Truth) is specific unity, said Plato, not the numerical multitude that holds the substance of things. Therefore he called Idea one and many, movable and immovable because as incorruptible species it is intelligible and one, and as it communicates itself to matter and is subject to movement and generation, it is sensible and many. In this second mode it has more of non-entity than of entity; seeing that it is one and another and is ever running but never diminishes. In the first mode it is an entity, and true. See now, the mathematicians take it for granted, that the true figures are not to be found in natural bodies, nor can they be there through the power either of nature or of art. Yon know, besides, that the truth (reality) of supernatural substances is above matter. We must therefore conclude that he who seeks the truth must rise above the reason of corporeal things. Besides which it must be considered, that he who feeds bas a certain natural memory of his food, especially when it is most required; it leaves in the mind the likeness and species of it, in an elevated manner, according to the elevation and glory of him who aims, and of that which is aimed at. Hence it is that everything has, innate, the intelligence of those things which belong to the conservation of the individual and species, and furthermore its final perfection depends upon efforts to seek its food through some kind of hunting or chase. Therefore it is necessary that the human soul should have the light, the genius, and the instruments suitable for its pursuit. And here contemplation comes to aid, and logic, the fittest mode for the pursuit of truth, to find it, to distinguish it, and to judge of it. So that one goes rambling amongst the wild woods of natural things, where there are many objects under shadow and mantle, for it is in a thick, dense, and deserted solitude that Truth most often has its secret cavernous retreat, all entwined with thorns and covered with bosky, rough and umbrageous plants; it is hidden, for the most part, for the most excellent and worthy reasons, buried and veiled with utmost diligence, just as we hide with the greatest care the greatest treasures, so that, sought by a great variety of hunters, of whom some are more able and expert, some less, it cannot be discovered without great labour.

Pythagoras went seeking for it with his imprints and vestiges impressed upon natural objects, which are numbers, the which display its progress, reasons, modes and operations in a certain manner, because in the number (of) multitude, the number (of) measures, and the number (of) moment or weight, the truth and Being are found in all things.

Anaxagoras and Empedocles considered that the omnipotent and all-producing divinity fills all things, and with them nothing was so small that it did not contain within it the occult in every respect, although they were always progressing onwards to where it was predominant, and where it found a more magnificent and elevated expression.

The Chaldeans sought for Truth by means of subtraction, not knowing how to affirm anything about it; and proceeded without these dogs of demonstrations and syllogisms, but solely forcing themselves to penetrate by removing and digging and clearing away by means of negations of every kind and discourses both open and secret.

Plato went twisting and turning and tearing to pieces and placing embankments so that the volatile and fugacious species should be as it were caught in a net and held behind the hedges of definitions, and he considered that superior things were, by participation, and according to similitude, reflected in those inferior, and these in those according to their greater dignity and excellence, and that the truth was in both the one and the other, according to a certain analogy, order and scale, in which the lowest of the superior order agrees with the highest of the inferior order. So that progress was from the lowest of nature to the highest, as from evil to good, from darkness to light, from the simple power to the simple action.

Aristotle boasts of being able to arrive at the desired booty by means of the imprints of tracks and vestiges, while he believes the effects will lead to the cause, although he, above all others who have occupied themselves with this sort of chase, has most deviated from the path, so as to be able hardly to distinguish the footsteps. Theologians there are, who, nourished in certain sects, seek the truth of nature in all her specific natural forms in which they see the eternal essence, the specific substantial perpetuator of the eternal generation and mutation of things, which are called after their founders and builders and above them all presides the form of forms, the fountain of light, very truth of very truth, God of gods, through whom all is full of divinity, truth, entity, goodness. This truth is sought as a thing inaccessible, as an object not to be objectized, incomprehensible. But yet, to no one does it seem possible to see the sun, the universal Apollo, the absolute light through supreme and most excellent species; but only its shadow, its Diana, the world, the universe, nature, which is in things, light which is in the opacity of matter, that is to say, so far as it shines in darkness.

Many then wander amongst the aforesaid paths of this deserted wood, very few are those who find the fountain of Diana. Many are content to hunt for wild beasts and things less elevated, and the greater number do not understand why, having spread their nets to the wind, they find their hands full of flies. Rare, I say, are the Actæons to whom fate has granted the power of contemplating the nude Diana and who, entranced with the beautiful disposition of the body of nature, and led by those two lights, the twin splendour of Divine goodness and beauty become transformed into stags; for they are no longer hunters, but that which is hunted. For the ultimate and final end of this sport, is to arrive at the acquisition of that fugitive and wild. body, so that the thief becomes the thing stolen, the hunter becomes the thing hunted; in all other kinds of sport, for special things, the hunter possesses himself of those things, absorbing them with the mouth of his own intelligence; but in that Divine and universal one, he comes to understand to such an, extent, that he becomes of necessity included, absorbed, united. Whence, from common, ordinary, civil, and popular, he becomes wild, like a stag, an inhabitant of the woods; he lives god-like under that grandeur of the forest; he lives in the simple chambers of the cavernous mountains, whence he beholds the great rivers; he vegetates intact and pure from ordinary greed, where the speech of the Divine converses more freely, to which so many men have aspired who longed to taste the Divine life while upon earth, and who with one voice have said: Ecce, elongavi fugiens, et mansi in solitudine. Thus the dogs--thoughts of Divine things---devour Actæon, making him dead to the vulgar and the crowd, loosened from the knots of perturbation of the senses, free from the fleshly prison of matter, whence they no longer see their Diana as thro So that he sees all as one; he sees no more by distinctions and numbers, which, according to the different senses, as through various cracks, cause to be seen and understood in confusion.

He sees Amphitrite, the source of all numbers, of all species, of all reasons, which is the monad, the real essence of the being of all, and if he does not see it in its essence, in absolute light, he sees it in its seed, which is like unto it, which is its image; for from the monad, which is the divinity, proceeds this monad which is nature, the universe, the world, where it is beheld and reflected, as the sun is in the moon by means of which it is illuminated; he finding himself in the hemisphere of intellectual substances. This is that Diana, that one who is the same entity, that entity which is comprehensible nature, in which burns the sun and the splendour of the higher nature, according to which, unity is both the generated and the generating, the producer and produced. Thus you can of yourself determine the mode, the dignity, and the success, which are most worthy of the hunter and the hunted. Therefore the enthusiast boasts of being the prey of Diana, to whom he rendered himself, and of whom he considers himself the accepted consort, and happy as a captive and a subject. Why, he envies no man (for there is none that can have more) or any other god that can have that species which is impossible to be obtained by an inferior nature, and therefore is not worthy to be desired, nor can one hunger after it.

CES. I have well understood all that you have said, and you have more than satisfied me. Now it is time to return home.

MAR. Well.

Third Dialogue

Interlocutors:
LIBERIO. LAODONIO.

LIB. Reclining in the shade of a cypress-tree, the enthusiast finding his mind free from other thoughts, it happened that the heart and the eyes spoke together as if they were animals and substances of different intellects and senses, and they made lament of that which was the beginning of his torment and which consumed his soul.

LAO. Repeat, if you eau recollect, the reasons and the words.

LIB. The heart began the dialogue, which, making itself heard by the breast, broke into these words

55. *First proposition of the heart to the eyes*.

How, eyes of mine, can that so much torment,
Which as an ardent fire from ye derives,
And which this mortal subject so afflicts
With unrelenting burning never spared?
Can ocean floods suffice to mitigate
The ardour of those flames? or slowest star
Within the frozen circle of the north
Offer umbrageous shade?
Ye took me captive, and the self-same hand
Doth hold me and reject me and through you
I in the body am: oat of it with the sun.
I am the source of life, yet am I not alive.
I know not what I am, for I belong
Unto this soul; but this soul is not mine.

LAO. Truly the hearing, the seeing, the knowing, is that which kindles desire, and therefore it is through the operation of the eyes that the heart becomes inflamed: and the more worthy the object which is present with them the stronger is the fire, and the more active are the flames. What then, must that kind be, for which the heart burns in such a way that the coldest star in the Arctic circle cannot cool it, nor can the whole body of water of the ocean stop its burning! What must be the excellence of that object that has made him an enemy to himself, a rebel to his own soul and content with such hostility and rebellion, although he be captive to one who despises and will have none of him! But let me hear whether the eyes made a response, and what they said.

LIB. They, on the other hand, complained of the heart as being the origin and cause why they shed, so many tears, and this was the sum of their proposition.

56. *First proposition of the eyes to the heart.*

How, oh my heart, do waters gush from thee
Like to the springs that bathe the Nereids' brows
Which daily in the sun are born and die?
Like to the double fountain of Amphitrite,
Which pours so great a flood across the earth,
That one might say, the gum of it exceeds
That of the stream which Egypt inundates,
Running its sevenfold course unto the sea.
Nature hath given two lights
To this small earth for governance;
But thou, perverter of eternal law,
Hast tamed them into everlasting streams.
But Heaven is not content to see her law
Decline before unbridled violence.

LAO. It is certain that the heart, grieved and stung, causes tears to spring to the eyes, and while these light the flames in this, that other dims those with moisture. But I am surprised at such exaggeration which says that the Nereids raising their wet faces to the eastern sun, is less than these waters (of the eyes). And more than that, they are equal to the ocean, not because they do pour, but because these two springing streams can pour such, and so much, that compared with them the Nile would appear a tiny stream divided into seven streamlets.

LIB. Be not surprised at that exaggeration nor at that potency without action! For you will understand all, after having heard the conclusion of their argument. Now listen how the heart responds to the proposition of the eyes.

LAO. I pray you, let me hear.
LIB.
57. *First response of the heart to the eyes.*

Eyes, if an immortal flame within me burn,
And I no other &m than burning fire;
If to come near me is to feel the blaze,
So that the heavens are fervid with my heat;
Why does my blazing flame consume you not,
But only contrary effects you feel?
Why saturated and not roasted ye,
If not of water but of fire I be?
Believe ye, oh ye blind,
That from such ardent burning is derived
The double passage, and those living founts
Have had their elements from Vulcan?
As force sometimes acquires a power
When by its contrary it is opposed.

You see that the heart could not persuade itself that from an opposite cause and beginning, could proceed a force of an opposite effect. So that it will not allow the possibility of it, except through antiperistasis, which means the strength which an opposite acquires from that which, flying from the other, comes to unite itself, incorporate itself, insphere itself, or concentrate itself towards the individual, through its own virtue, which, the farther it is removed from the dimensions (dimensioni) the more efficacious it becomes.

LAO. Tell me, how did the eyes respond to the heart?

58. *First response of the eyes to the heart.*

Thy passion does confuse thee, oh my heart,
The path of truth thou hast entirely lost;
That which in us is seen--that which is hid--
Is seed of oceans. Neptune, if by fate
His kingdom he should lose, would find it here entire.
How does the burning flame from us derive
Who of the sea the double parent are?
So senseless thou'rt become!
Dost thou believe the flame will pass
And leave the doors all wet behind
That thou may'st feel the ardour of the same?
As splendour through a glass, dost thou
Believe that it through us will penetrate?

Now I will not begin to philosophize about the identity of opposites which I have studied in the book De Principio ed uno, and I will suppose that which is usually received, that the opposites in the same genus are quite separate (distantissimi), so that the meaning of this response is more easily learned where the eyes call themselves the seed or founts in the virtual potentiality of which is the sea; so that if Neptune should lose all the waters, he could recall them into action by their own potentiality, where they are as in the beginning, medium and material. But it is not urged as a necessity, when they say it cannot be, that the flame passes over to the heart through their room (stanza e cortile) and courtyard leaving so many waters behind, for two reasons. First, because such an impediment cannot exist in action. if (equally?) violent opposition is not put into action; second, because in so far as the waters are actually in the eyes, they can give passage to the heat as to the light; for experience proves that the luminous ray kindles, by means of reflection, any material that becomes opposed to it, without heating the glass; and the ray passes through a glass, crystal or other vase, full of water, and heats an object placed under it, without heating the thick intervening body. As it is also true that it causes dry and dusty impressions in the caves of the deep sea. Therefore by analogy, if not by the same sort of reasons, we may see how it is possible that, through the lubricant and dark passage of the eyes, the affection may be kindled and inflamed by that light, the which for the same reason cannot be in the middle. As the light of the sun, according to other reasoning, is in the middle air, or again in the nearer sense, and again in the common sense, or again in the intellect, not withstanding that from one mode proceeds the other mode of being.

LAO. Are there anymore discourses?

LIB. Yes; because both the one and the other are trying to find out in what way it is that it (the heart) contains so many flames and those (the eyes) so many waters. The heart then makes the next proposition.

59. *Second proposition of the heart to the eyes.*

If to the foaming sea the rivers run,
And pour their streams into the sea's dark gulf,

How does the kingdom of the water-gods,
Fed by the double torrent of these eyes,
Increase not; since the earth
Must lose the glorious overflow?
How is it that we do not see the day,
When from the mount Deukalion returns?
Where are the lengthening shores,
Where is the torrent to put out my flame,
Or, failing this, to give it greater power?
Does drop of water ever fall to earth
In such a way as leads me to suppose
It is not as the senses show it?

  It asks, what power is this, which is not put into action? If the waters are so many, why does Neptune not come to tyrannize over the kingdoms of the other elements? Where are the inundated banks? Where is he who will give coolness to the ardent fire? Where is the drop of water by which I may affirm through the eyes that which the senses deny? But the eyes in the same way ask another question.

  60. *Second proposition of the eyes to the heart.*

  If matter changed and turned to fire acquires
The movement of a lighter element,
Rising aloft unto the highest heaven;
Wherefore, ignited by the fire of love,
Swifter than wind, dost thou not rise and flash
Into the sun and be incorporate there?
Why rather stay a pilgrim here below
Than open through the air and us a way?
No spark of fire from that heart
Goes out through the wide atmosphere.
Body of dust and ashes is not seen,
Nor water-laden smoke ascends on high.
All is contained entire within itself,
And not of flame, is reason, sense, or thought.

  LAO. This proposition is neither more nor less conclusive than the other. But let us come at once to the answers if there be any.

  LIC. There are some certainly and full of sap. Listen.

  61. *Second response of the heart to the eyes.*

He is a fool, who that alone believes,
Which to the sense appears, who reason scorns.
My flame could never wing its way above.
The conflagration infinite remains unseen.
Between the eyes their waters are contained,
One infinite encroaches not upon another.
Nature wills not that all should perish.
If so much fire's enough for so much sphere,
Say, say, oh eyes,
What shall we do? how act
In order to make known, or I, or you,
For its deliverance, the sad plight of the soul?
If one and other of us both be bid,
How can we move the beauteous god to pity?

LAS. If it is not true it is very well imagined if it is not so. it is yet a very good excuse the one for the other; because where there are two forces, of the which one is not greater than the other, the operation of both must cease, for one resists as much as the other insists, and one assails while the other defends. If therefore the sea is infinite and the force of tears in the eyes is immense, it never can be made apparent by speech, nor the impetus of the fire concealed in the heart break forth, nor can they (the eyes) send forth the twin torrent to the sea if the heart shelters them with equal tenacity. Therefore the beautiful deity cannot be expected to be pitiful towards the afflicted soul because of the exhibition of tears which distil from the eyes, or speech which breaks forth from the breast.

LIB. Now note the answer of the eyes to this Proposition:--

62. *Second response of the eyes to the heart.*

Alas! we poured into the wavy sea,
The strength of our two founts in vain,
For two opposing powers hold it conceded,
Lest it go rolling aimlessly adown.
The strength unmeasured of the burning heart,
Withholds a passage to the lofty streams;
Barring their twofold course unto the sea,
Nature abhors the covered ground.
Now say, afflicted heart, what canst thou bring

To oppose against us with an equal force?
Oh, where is he, will boast himself to be
Exalted by this most unhappy love,
If of thy pain and mine it can be said,
The greater they, the less it may be seen.

Both these evils being infinite, like two equally vigorous opposites they curb and suppress each other: it could not be so if they were both finite, seeing that a precise equality does not belong to natural things, nor would it be so if the one were finite, the other infinite; for of a certainty the one would absorb the other, and they would both be seen, or, at least one, through the other. Beneath these sentences, there lies hidden, ethical and natural philosophy, and I leave it to be searched for, meditated upon and understood, by whosoever will and can. This alone I will not leave (unsaid) that it is not without reason that the affection of the heart is said to be the infinite sea by the apprehension of the eyes. For the object of the mind being infinite, and no definite object being proposed to the intellect, the will cannot be satisfied by a finite good, but if besides that, something else, is found, it is desired and sought for; for, as is commonly said, the apex of the inferior species is the beginning of the superior species, whether the degrees are taken according to the forms, the which we cannot consider as being infinite, or according to the modes and reasons of those, in which way, the highest good being infinite, it would be supposed to be infinitely communicated, according to the condition of the things, over which it is diffused. However, there is no definite species of the universe. I speak according to the figure and mass; there is no definite species of the intellect; the affections are not a definite species.

LAO. These two powers of the soul, then, never we nor can be perfect for the object, if they refer to it infinitely?

LIB. So it would be if this infinite were by negative privation or privative negation of the end, as it is for a more positive affirmation of the end, infinite and endless.

LAO. You mean, then, two kinds of affinity; the one privative, the which may be towards something which is power, as, infinite is darkness, the end of which is the position of light; the other perfecting, which tends to the act and perfection, as infinite is the light, the end of which would be privation and darkness. In this, then, the intellect conceives the light, the good, the beautiful, in so far as the horizon of its capacity extends, and the soul, which drinks of Divine nectar and the fountain of eternal life in so far as its own vessel allows, and one sees that the light is beyond the circumference of his horizon, where it can go and penetrate more and more, and the nectar and fount of living water is infinitely fruitful, so that it can become over more and more intoxicated.

LIB. From this it does not follow that there is imperfection in the object, nor that there is little satisfaction in the potency, but that the power is included in the object and beatifically absorbed by it. Here the eyes imprint upon the heart, that is upon the intelligence, and rouse in the will an infinite torment of love, where there is no pain because nothing is sought which is not obtained; but it is happiness, because that which is there sought is always found, and there is no satiety, inasmuch as there is always appetite, and therefore enjoyment; in this it is not like the food of the body, the which with satiety loses enjoyment, has no pleasure before the enjoyment, nor after enjoyment, but only in the enjoyment itself, and where it passes certain limits it comes to feel annoyance and disgust. Behold, then, in a certain analogy, how the highest good ought to be also infinite, in order that it should not some time turn to evil; as food, which is good for the body, if it is not limited, may come to be poison. Thus it is that the water of the ocean does not extinguish that flame, and the rigour of the Arctic circle does not mitigate that ardour. Therefore it is bad through (the) one hand, which holds him and rejects him it holds him, because it has him for its own; it rejects him because, flying from him, the higher it makes itself the more he, ascends upwards to it; the more he follows it, the farther off it appears, by reason of its high excellence, according as it is said: Accedit homo, ad cor altum, et exaltabitur Deus. Such blessedness of affection begins in this life, and in, this state it has its mode of being. Hence the heart can say that it is within with the body, and without with the sun, in so far as the soul with its twin faculty, puts into operation two functions: the one to vivify and realize the animal body, the other to contemplate superior things; so that it is in receptive potentiality from above, as it is in re-active potentiality below, towards the body. The body is, as it were, dead, and as it were apart from the soul, the which is its life and its perfection; and the soul is as it were dead, and a thing apart from the superior illuminating intelligence, from which the intellect is derived as to its nature and acts. Therefore, the heart is said to be the beginning of life, and not to be alive, it is said. to belong to the animating soul, and that this does not belong to it; because it is inflamed by Divine love, and finally converted into fire, which can set on fire that which comes near it, seeing that it has contracted into itself the divinity; it is made god, and consequently in its kind it can inspire others with love; as the splendour of the sun may be seen and admired in the moon. And as for that which belongs to the consideration of the eyes, know, that in the present discourse they have two functions; one to impress the heart, the other to receive the impression of the heart; as this also has two functions, one to receive the impressions from the eyes, the other to impress them. The eyes study the species and propose them to the heart; the heart desires them, and presents his desire to the eyes; these conceive the light, disease it, and kindle the fire in the heart, which heated and kindled, sends its waters (umore) to them, so that they may dispose of them (digeriscano). Thus, firstly, cognition moves the affection, and soon the affection moves the cognition. The eyes, when they move (the heart), are dry, because they perform the office of a looking-glass, and of a representer; when they are moved however, they become troubled and perturbed, because they perform the office of a diligent executer, seeing that with the speculating intellect, the beautiful and the good is first seen, then the will desires it; and later the industrious intellect procures it, follows it, and seeks it. Tearful eyes signify the. difficulty of separating the thing wished for from the wisher, the which in order that it should not pall, nor disgust, presents itself as an infinite longing(studio) which ever has, and ever seeks; seeing that the delight of the gods is ascribed to drinking, not to having tasted ambrosia, and to the continual enjoyment of food and drink, and not in being satiated and without desire for them. Hence they have satiety as it were in movement and apprehension, not in quiet and comprehension; they are not satiated without appetite, nor are they in a state of desire, without being in a certain way satiated.

LAO. Esuries satiata, satietas esuriens.

LIB. Precisely so.

LAO: From this I can comprehend how, without blame, but with great truth and understanding, it has been said that Divine love weeps with indescribable, groans, because having all it loves all, and, loving all has all.

LIB. But many comments would be necessary if we would understand that Divine love which is. deity itself; and one easily understands Divine love, so far as it is to be found in its effects and in the inferior nature. I do not say that which from the divinity is diffused into things, but that of things which aspires to the divinity.

LAO. Now of this and of other matters we will discourse more at our ease presently. Let us go.

Fourth Dialogue.

Interlocutors:
SEVERINO. MINUTOLO.

SEV. You will see the origin of the nine blind men, who state nine reasons and special causes of their blindness, and yet they all agree in one general reason and one common enthusiasm.

MIN. Begin with the first!

SEV. The first of these, notwithstanding that he is blind by nature, yet he laments, saying to the others, that he cannot persuade himself that nature has been less courteous to them than to him; seeing that although they do not (now) see, yet they have enjoyed sight, and have had experience of that sense, and of the value of that faculty, of which they have been deprived, while he came into the world as a mole, to be seen and not to see, to long for the sight of that which he never had seen.

MIN. Many have fallen in love through report alone.

SEV. They have, says he, the happiness of retaining that Divine image present in the mind, so that, although blind, they have in imagination that which he cannot have. Then in the sistine he turns to his guide and begs him to lead him to some precipice, so that he may no longer endure this contempt and persecution of nature. He says then:

63. *The first blind man.*
Ye now afflicted are, who erst were glad,
For ye, have lost the light that once was yours,
Yet happy, for ye have the twin lights known.
These eyes ne'er lighted were, and ne'er were quenched;
But a more grievous destiny is mine
Which calls for heavier lamentation.
Who will deny that nature upon me
Has frowned more harshly than on you?
Conduct me to the precipice, my guide,
And give me peace, for there will I a cure
For this my dolour and affliction find;
For to be seen, yet not to see the light,

Like an incapable and sightless mole,
Is to be useless and a burden on the earth

Now follows the other, who, bitten by the serpent of jealousy, became affected in the organ of sight. He wanders without any guide, unless he has jealousy for his escort. He begs some of the bystanders, that seeing there is no remedy for his misfortune, they should have pity upon him, so that he should no longer feel it; that he might become as unmanifest to himself as he is to the light, and that they bury him together with his own misfortune. He says then:

64. *The second blind man.*

Alecta has torn from out her dreadful hair,
The infernal worm that with a cruel bite,
Has fiercely fastened on my soul,
And of my senses, torn the chief away,
Leaving the intellect without its guide.
la vain the soul some consolation seeks.
That spiteful, rabid, rancorous jealousy
Makes me go stumbling along the way.
If neither magic spell nor sacred plant,
Nor virtue hid in the enchanter's stone,
Will yield me the deliverance that I ask:
Let one of you, my friends, be pitiful,
And put me out, as are put out my eyes,
That they and. I together be entombed.

The other follows, who says that he became blind through having been suddenly brought out of the darkness into a great light accustomed to behold ordinary beauties, a celestial beauty was suddenly presented before his eyes--a sun-god--in this manner his sight became dull and the twin lights which shine at the prow of the soul were put out: for the eyes are like two beacons, which guide the ship, and this would happen to one brought up in Cimmerian obscurity if he fixed his eyes suddenly upon the sun. In the sistine he begs for free passage to Hades, because darkness alone is suitable to a dark condition. He says:

65. *The third blind man.*

If sudden on the sight, the star of day
Should shed his beams on one in darkness reared,

Nurtured beneath the black Cimmerian sky,
Far from the radiance of the glorious sun
The double light, the beacon of the soul
He quenches. then as a foe he hides.
Thus were my eyes made dull, inept,
Used only, wonted beauties to behold.
Conduct me to the land where darkness reigns!
Wherefore being dead, speak I amidst the folk?
A chip of Hell, why do I mix and move
Amongst the living, wherefore do I drink
The hated. air, since all my pain
Is clue to having seen the highest good?

    The fourth blind man comes forward, not blind for the same reason as the former one. For as that one was blinded through the sudden aspect of the light, this one is so, from having too frequently beheld it, or through having fixed his eyes too much upon it, so that he has lost the sense of all other light, but he does not consider himself to be blind through looking at that one which has blinded him: and the same may be said of the sense of sight as of the sense of hearing, that those whose ears are accustomed to great noises, do not hear the lesser, as is well known of those who live near the cataracts of the great river Nile which fall precipitously down to the plain.

    MIN. Thus, all those who have accustomed the body and the soul to things more difficult and great, are not apt to feel annoyed by smaller difficulties. So that fellow ought not to be discontented about his blindness.

    SEV. Certainly not. But one says, voluntarily blind, of one who desires that every other thing be hidden because it annoys him to be diverted from looking at that which alone he wishes to behold. Meanwhile he prays the passers-by to prevent his coming to mischief in any encounter, while he goes so absorbed and captivated by one principal object.

    MIN. Repeat his words!

    SEV. He says:

66. *The fourth blind man*.

Headlong from on high to the abyss,
The cataract of the Nile falls down and dulls the senses

Of the joyless folk to every other sound,
So stood I too, with spirit all intent
Upon. the living light, that lights the world;
Dead henceforth to all the lesser splendours,
While that light shines, let every other thing
Be to the voluntary blind concealed.
I pray you save me stumbling 'mongst the stones,
Make me aware of the wild beast,
Show me whether up or down I go;
So that the miserable bones fall not,
Into a low and cavernous place,
While I, without a guide, am stepping on.

    To the blind man that follows, it happens that having wept so much, his eyes are become dim, so that he is not able to extend the visual ray, so as to distinguish visible objects, nor can he see the light, which in spite of himself, through so many sorrows, he at one time was able to see. Besides which he considers that his blindness is not from constitution, but from habit, and is peculiar to himself, because the luminous fire which kindles the soul in the pupil, was for too long a time and with too much force, repressed and restrained by a contrary humour, so that although he might cease from weeping, he cannot be persuaded that this would result in the longed-for vision. You will hear what he says to the throng in order that they should enable him to proceed on his way:

    67. *The fifth blind man.*

    Eyes of mine, with waters ever full,
When will the bright spark of the visual ray,
Darting, spring through each veiling obstacle,
That I may see again those holy lights
That were the alpha of my darling pain?
Ah, woe! I fear me it is quite extinct,
So long oppressed and conquered by its opposite.
Let the blind man pass on!
And turn your eyes upon these founts
Which overcome the others one and all.
Should any dare dispute it with me,
There's one would surely answer him again;
That in one eye of mine an ocean is contained.

The sixth blind man is sightless because, through so much weeping, there remains no more moisture, not even the crystalline and moisture through which, as a diaphanous medium, the visual ray was transmitted, and the external light and visible species were introduced, so that the heart became compressed because all the moist substance, whose office it is to keep united the various parts and opposites, was absorbed, and the amorous affection remains without the effect of tears. Therefore the organ is destroyed through the victory of the other elements, and it is consequently left without sight and without consistency of the parts of the body altogether. He then proposes to the bystanders that which you shall hear:

68. *The sixth blind man.*

Eyes, no longer eyes, fountains no longer founts,
Ye have wept out the waters that did keep
The body, soul, and spirit joined in one,
And thou, reflecting crystal, which from without
So much unto the soul made manifest,
Thou art consumed by the wounded heart.
So towards the dark and cavernous abyss,
I, a blind and man, direct my steps.
Ah, pity me, and do not hesitate
To help my speedy going. I who
So many rivers in the dark days spread out,
Finding my only comfort in my tears,
Now that my streams and fountains all are dry,
Towards profound oblivion lead the way.

The next one avers that he has lost his sight through the intensity of the flame, which, proceeding from the heart, first destroyed the eyes, and then dried up all the remaining moisture of the substance of the lover, so that being all melted and turned to flame, he is no longer himself, because the fire whose property it is to resolve all bodies into their atoms, has converted him into impalpable dust, whereas by virtue of water alone, the atoms of other bodies thicken, and are welded together to make a substantial composition. Yet he is not deprived of the sense of the most intense flame. Therefore, in the sistine he would have space made for him to pass; for if anybody should be touched by his fires he would become such that he would have no more feeling of the flames of hell, for their heat would be to him as cold snow.

69. *The seventh blind man.*

Beauty, which through the eyes rushed to the heart,
And formed the mighty furnace in my breast,
Absorbing first the visual moisture; then,
Spouting aloft its grasping flashing flame,
Devouring every other fluid,
To set the dryer element at rest,
Has thus reduced me to a boneless dust,
Which now to its own atoms is resolved.
If anguish infinite your fears should rouse
Make space, give way, oh peoples!
Beware of my fierce penetrating fire,
For if it should invade and touch you, ye
Would feel and know the fires of hell
To be like winter's cold.

The eighth follows, whose blindness is caused by the dart which love has caused to penetrate from the eyes to the heart. Hence, he laments not only as being blind, but furthermore because he is wounded and burnt so fiercely, that he believes no other can be equally so. The sense of it is easily expressed in this sonnet:--

70. *The eighth blind man.*

Vile onslaught, evil struggle, unrighteous palm,
Fine point, devouring fire, strong nerve,
Sharp wound, impious ardour, cruel body,
Dart, fire and tangle of that wayward god
Who pierced the eyes, inflamed the heart, bound the soul,
Made me at once sightless, a lover, and a slave,
So that, blind I have at all times, in all ways and places,
The feeling of my wound, my fire, my noose.
Men, heroes, and gods!
Who be on earth, or near to Ditis or to Jove,
I pray ye say, when, how, and where did ye
Feel ever, hear, or see in any place
Woes like to these, amongst the oppressed
Amongst the damned, 'mongst lovers?

Finally comes the last one, who is also mute through not having been able, or having dared, to say that which he most desired to say, for fear of offending or exciting contempt, and he is deprived of speaking of every other thing: therefore, it is not he who speaks, but his guide who relates the affair, about which I do not speak, but only bring you the sense thereof:

71. *The guide of the ninth blind man.*

Happy are ye, oh all ye sightless lovers,
That ye the reason of your pains can tell,
By virtue of your tears you can be sure
Of pure and favourable receptions.
Amongst you all, the latent fire of him
Whose guide I am, rages most fiercely,
Though he is mute for want of boldness
To make known his sorrows to his deity.
Make way! open ye wide the way,
Be ye benign unto this vacant face,
Oh people full of grievous hindrances,
The while this harassed. weary trunk
Goes knocking at the doors
To meet a death less painful, more profound.

Here are mentioned nine reasons, which are the cause that the human mind is blind as regards the Divine object and cannot fix its eyes upon it. And of these, the first, allegorized through the first blind man, is the quality of its own species, which in so far as the degree in which he finds himself admits, he aspires certainly higher, than he is able to comprehend.

MIN. Because no natural desire is vain, we are able to assure ourselves of a more excellent state which is suitable to the soul outside of this body, in the which it may be possible to unite itself, or to approach more nearly, to its object.

SEV. Thou sayest well that no natural impulse or power is without strong reason; it is in fact the same rule of nature which orders things. So far, it is a thing most true and most certain to well-disposed intellects, that the human soul, whatever it may show itself while it is in the body, that same, which it makes manifest in this state, is the expression of its pilgrim existence in this region; because it aspires to the truth and to universal good, and is not satisfied with that which comes on account of and to the profit of its species.

The second, represented by the second blind man, proceeds from some troubled affection, as in the question of Love and Jealousy, the which is like a moth, which has the same subject, enemy and father, that is, it consumes the cloth or wood from which it is generated.

MIN. This does not seem to me to take place with heroic love.

SEV. True, according to the same reason which is. seen in the lower kind of love; but I mean according to another reason similar to that which happens to those who love truth and goodness. which shows itself when they are angry against those who adulterate it, spoil it, or corrupt it, or who in other ways would treat it with indignity, as has been the case with those who have brought themselves to suffer death and pains, and to being ignominiously treated by ignorant peoples and vulgar sects.

MIN. Certainly no one truly loves the truth and the good who is not angry against the multitude; as no one loves in the ordinary way who is not jealous and fearful about the thing loved.

SEV. And so he comes to be really blind in many things, and according to the common opinion he is quite infatuated and mad.

MIN. I have noted a place which says that all those are infatuated and mad, who have sense beyond and outside of the general sense of other men. But such extravagance is of two kinds, according as one goes beyond and ascends up higher than the greater number rise or can rise, and these are they who are inspired with Divine enthusiasm; or by going down lower where those are found who have greater defect of sense and of reason than the many, and the ordinary; but in that kind of madness, insensibility and blindness, will not be found the jealous hero.

SEV. Although be is told that much learning makes him mad, yet no one can really abuse him. The third, represented by the third blind man, proceeds from this: that Divine Truth according to supernatural reasoning, called metaphysics, manifests itself to those few to whom it shows itself, and does not proceed with measure of movement and time as occurs in the physical sciences, that is, those which are acquired by natural light, the which, in discoursing of a thing known to reason by means of the senses, proceed to the knowledge of another thing, unknown, the which discourse is called argument; but immediately and suddenly, according to the method which belongs to such efficiency. 'Whence a divine has said: "Attenuati sunt oculi mei suspicientes in excelsum." So that it does not require a useless lapse of time, fatigue, and study, and inquisitorial act to have it, but it is taken in quickly, as the solar light, without hesitation, and makes itself present to whoever turns himself to it. and opens himself to it.

MIN. Do you mean then, that the student and the philosopher are not more apt to receive this light than the ignorant?

SEV. In a certain way no, and in a certain way yes. There is no difference, when the Divine mind through its providence comes to communicate itself without disposition of the subject; I mean to say when it communicates itself because it seeks and elects its subject; but there is a great difference, when it waits and would be sought, and then according to its own good will and pleasure it makes itself to be found. In this way it does not appear to all, nor can it appear to others, than to those who seek it. Hence it is said, "Qui quærunt, me, invenient me;" and again--"Qui sitit, veniat et bibat!"

MIN. It is not to be denied, that the apprehension of the second manner is made in Time. (Comes with time?)

SEV. You do not distinguish between the disposition towards the Divine light and the apprehension of the same. Certainly I do not deny that it requires time to dispose oneself, discourse, study and fatigue; but as we say that change takes place in time, and generation in an instant, and as we see that with time, the windows are opened, but the sun enters in a moment, so does it happen similarly in this case.

The fourth, represented in the following, is not really unworthy, like that which results from the habit of believing in the false opinions of the vulgar, which are very far removed from the opinions of philosophers, and are derived from the study of vulgar philosophies, which are by the multitude considered the more true, the more they appeal to common sense. And this habit is one of the greatest and strongest disadvantages, because as Alcazele and Averroes showed, it is like that which happens to those persons who from childhood and youth are in the habit of eating poison, and have become such, that it is converted into sweet and proper nutriment, and on the other hand, they abominate those things which are really good and sweet according to common nature; but it is most worthy, because it is founded upon the habit of looking at the true light; the which habit cannot come into use for the multitude, as we have said. This blindness is heroic, and is of such a kind that it can worthily satisfy the present heroic blind man, who is so far from troubling himself about it that he is able to explain every other sight, and he would crave nothing else from the community save a free passage and progress in contemplation, for he finds himself usually hampered and blocked by obstacles and opposition.

The fifth results from the disproportion of the means of our cognition to the knowable; seeing that in order to contemplate Divine things, the eyes must be opened by means of images, analogies and other reasonings which by the Peripatetics are comprehended under the name of fancies (fantasmi); or, by means of Being, to proceed to speculate about Essence, by means of its effects and the knowledge of the cause; the which means, are so far from ensuring the attainment of such an end, that it is easier to believe that the highest and most profound cognition of Divine things, is through negation and not through affirmation, knowing that the Divine beauty and goodness is not that which can or does fall within our conception, but that which is above and beyond, incomprehensible; chiefly in that condition called by the philosopher speculation of phantoms, and by the theologian, vision through analogies, reflections and enigmas, because we see, not the true effects and the true species of things, or the substance of ideas, but the shadows, vestiges and simulacra of them, like those who are inside the cave and have from their birth their shoulders turned away from the entrance of the light, and their faces towards the end, where they do not see that which is in reality, but the shadows of that which is found substantially outside the cave. Therefore by the open vision which it has lost, and knows it has lost, a spirit similar to or better than that of Plato weeps, desiring exit from the cave. whence, not through reflexion, but through immediate conversion he may see the light again.

MIN. It appears to me that this blind man does not refer to the difficulty which proceeds from reflective vision, but to that which is caused through the medium between the visual power and the object.

SEV. These two modes, although they are distinct in the sensitive cognition, or ocular vision, at the same time are united together in the rational or intellectual cognition.

MIN. It seems to me that I have heard and read that in every vision. the means, or the intermediary is required between the power and the object. Because as by means of the light diffused in the air and the figure of the thing, which in a certain way proceeds from that which is seen, to that which sees, the act of seeing is put into effect, so in the intellectual region, where shines the sun of the intellect, acting between the intelligible species formed as proceeding from the object, our intellect comes to comprehend something of the divinity, or something inferior to it. Because, as our eye, when we see, does not receive the light of the fire and of gold, in substance, but in similitude; so the intellect, in whatever state it is found, does not receive the divinity substantially, so that there should be substantially as many gods as there are intelligences, but in similitude; therefore they are not formally gods, but denominatively divine, the divinity and Divine beauty being one, exalted above all things.

SEV. You say well; but for all your well saying, there is no need for me to retract, because I have never said the contrary. But I must declare and explain. Therefore, first I maintain that the immediate vision, so called and understood by us, does not do away with that sort of medium which is the intelligible species, nor that which is the light; but that which is equal to the thickness and density of the crystalline or opaque intermediate body; as happens to him who sees by means of the waters more or less turbid, or air foggy and cloudy, who would believe he was looking as without a medium when it was conceded to him to look through the pure air, light and clear, All which you have explained where it says:

"When will the bright spark of the visual ray Darting, spring through each veiling obstacle."

[paragraph continues] But let us return. The sixth, represented in the following, is caused only by the imbecility and unreality of the body, which is in continual motion, mutation, and change, the operations of which must follow the condition of its faculty, the which is a result of the condition of its nature and being. How can immobility, reality, entity, truth be contained in that which is ever different, and always makes and is made, other and otherwise? What, truth, what picture can be painted and impressed, where the pupils of the eyes are dispersed in water, the water into steam, the steam into flame, the flame into air, and this in other and other without end: the subject of sense and cognition turns for ever upon the wheel of mutation?

MIN. Movement is change, and that which is changeable works and operates ever differently, because the conception and affection follow the reason and condition of the subject; and he who sees other and other different and differently must, necessarily be blind as regards that beauty which is one and alone and is the same unity and entity.

SEV. So it is. The seventh, contained allegorically in the sentiment of the seventh blind man, is the result of the fire of the affections, whence some become impotent and incapable of comprehending the truth, by making the affection precede the intellect. There are those who love before they understand: whence it happens that all things appear to them according to the colour of their affections, whereas he who would understand the truth by means of contemplation, ought to be perfectly pure in thought.

MIN. In truth, one sees how much diversity there is in meditators and inquirers, because some, according to their habits and early fundamental discipline, proceed by means of numbers, others by means of images, others by means of order and disorder, others through composition and division, others by separation and congregation, others by inquiry and doubt, others by discussions and definitions, others by interpretations and decypherings, of voices, words, and dialects, so that some are mathematical philosophers, some metaphysicians, others logicians, others grammarians; so there are divers contemplators, who with different affections set themselves to study and apply the meaning of written sentences; whence we find that the same light of truth, expressed in the selfsame book, serves with the same words the proposition of so numerous, diverse, and contrary sects.

SEV. That is to say, that the affections are very powerful in hindering the comprehension of the Truth, notwithstanding that the person may not himself perceive it; just as it happens to a stupid invalid who does not say that his mouth is bittered but that the food is bitter. Now that kind of blindness is expressed by him whose eyes are changed and deprived of their natural powers, by that which the heart has given and imprinted upon it, powerful not only to change the sense, but besides that, all the faculties of the soul as the present image shows. According to the meaning of the eighth, the high intelligible object has blinded the intellect, as the high superposed sensible has corrupted the senses. Thus it would happen to him who should see Jove in his majesty, he would lose his life and in consequence his senses. As he who looks aloft sometimes is overcome by the majesty. Besides, when he comes to penetrate the Divine species, he passes it like a ray. Whence say the theologians that the Divine word is more penetrating than sharp point of sword or knife. Hence is derived the form and impression of His own footstep, upon which nothing else can be imprinted and sealed. Therefore, that form being there confirmed and the new strange one not being able to take its place unless the other yields, consequently he can say, that he has no power of taking any other, if there is one who replaces it or scatters it through the necessary want of proportion. The ninth reason is exemplified, by the ninth who is blind through want of confidence, through dejection of spirit, the which is caused and brought about also by a great love which He fears to offend by His temerity. Whence says the Psalm: "Averte oculos tuos a me, quia ipsi me avolare fecere." And so he suppresses his eyes so as not to see that which most of all he desires, as he keeps his tongue from talking with whom he most wishes to speak, from fear that a defective look or word should humiliate him or bring him in some way into misfortune. And this generally proceeds from the apprehension of the excellence of the object above its potential faculty whence the most profound and divine theologians say, that God is more honoured and loved by silence than by words; as one sees more by shutting the eyes O the species represented, than by opening them, therefore the negative theology of Pythagoras and Dionysius is more celebrated than the demonstrative theology of Aristotle and the scholastic doctors.

MIN. Let us go, and we will reason by the way.

SEV. As you please.

Fifth Dialogue.

Interlocutors:
LAODOMIA. GIULIA.

LAO. Some other time, oh my sister, thou wilt hear what happened to those nine blind men, who were at first nine most beautiful and amorous youths, who being so inspired by the loveliness of your face, and having no hope of receiving the reward of their love, and fearing that such despair would reduce them to final ruin, went away from the happy Campanian country, and of one accord, those who at first were rivals for your beauty, swore not to separate until they had tried in all possible ways to find something more beautiful than you or at least equal to you; besides which, that they might discover that mercy and pity which they could not find in your breast armed with pride; for they believed this was the only remedy which could bring them out of that cruel captivity. The third day after their solemn departure, as they were passing by the Circean mount, it pleased them to go and see those antiquities, the cave and fane of that goddess. When they were come there, the majesty of the solitary place, the high, storm-beaten rocks, the murmur of the sea waves which break amongst those caves, and many other circumstances of the locality and the season combined, made them feel inspired; and one of them I will tell thee, more bold than the others, spoke these words: "Oh might it please heaven that in these days, as in the past more happy ages, some wise Circe might make herself present who, with plants and minerals working her incantations, would be able to curb nature. I should believe that she, however proud, would surely be pitiful unto our woes. She, solicited by our supplications and laments, would condescend either to give a remedy or to concede a grateful vengeance for the cruelty of our enemy."

Hardly had he finished uttering these words than there became visible to them a palace, which, whoever had knowledge of human things, could easily comprehend that it was not the work of man, nor of nature; the form and manner of it I will explain to thee another time. Whence, filled with great wonder and touched by hope that some propitious deity, who must have placed this before them, would explain their condition and fortunes, they said. with one accord they could meet with nothing worse than death, which they considered a less evil than to live in so much anguish. Therefore they entered, not finding any door that was shut against them nor janitor who questioned them. They found themselves in a very richly ornamented room, where with royal majesty, (as one may say, Apollo was found again by Phaeton;) appears she, who if; called his daughter, and at whose appearance they saw vanish all the figures of many other deities who ministered unto her. Then, received and comforted by this gracious face, they advanced, and overcome by the splendour of that majesty, they bent their knee to the earth, and altogether, with the diversity of tones which their various genius suggested, they laid open their vows to the goddess. By her finally, they were treated in such a manner that, blind and homeless, with great labour having ploughed the seas, passed over rivers, overcome mountains, traversed plains for the space of ten years, and at the end of which time having arrived under that temperate sky of the British Isles, and come into the presence of the lovely, graceful nymphs of Father Thames, they (the nine), having made humble obeisance, and the nymphs having received them with acts of purest courtesy, one, the principal amongst them, who later on will be named, with tragic and lamenting accents laid bare the common cause in this manner:

Of those, oh gentle Dames, who with closed urn,
Present themselves, whose hearts am pierced
Not for a fault by nature caused,
But through a cruel fate,
That in a living death,
Does hold them fast, we each and all are blind.
    Nine spirits are we, wandering many years,
Longing to know; and many lands
O'ertravelled, one day were surprised
By a sore accident,
To which if you attend,
You'll say, oh worthy, oh unhappy lovers!
    An impious Circe, who presumes to boast
Of having for her sire this glorious sun,

Welcomed us after many wanderings:
Opened a certain urn,
With water sprinkled us,
And to the sprinkling added an enchantment.
     Waiting the finish of this work of hers
We all were quiet, mute, attent,
Until she said, "Oh ye unhappy ones,
Blind be ye all,
Gather that fruit
Those get who fix their thoughts on things above."
     Daughter and Mother of horror and darkness and woe
They cried, who sudden were struck blind,
It pleased you then, so proud and harsh,
To treat these wretched lovers,
Who put themselves before you,
Ready to consecrate to you their hearts.
     But when the sudden fury somewhat stayed,
Which this new case had brought on them,
Each one within himself withdrew,
While rage to grief gave place;
To her they turned for pity,
With chosen words companioning their tears.
     Now if it please thee, gracious sorceress,
If zeal for glory chance to move thy heart,
Or milk of kindness soften it,
Be merciful to us,
And with thy magic herbs,
Heal up the wound imprinted on our hearts.
     If wish to succour rules thy beauteous hand,
Make no delay, lest some of as
Unhappy ones reach death, ere we
Praising thy act
Can each one say,
So much did she torment, yet more did heal.
     Then she replied: Oh curious prying minds,
Take this my other fatal urn,
Which my own hand may not unclose;
Over the wide expanse of earth,

Wander ye still,
Search for and visit all the various kingdoms.
      Fate hath decreed, it ne'er shall be unclosed
Till lofty wisdom, noble chastity
And loveliness with these combined,
Shall set their hands to it;
All other efforts vain,
To make this fluid open to the sky.
      Then should it chance to sprinkle beauteous hands,
Of those who come anear for remedy,
Its god-like virtues you may prove,
And turning cruel pain
Into a sweet content,
Two lovely stars upon the earth you'll see.
      Meanwhile be none of you cast down or sad,
Although long while in deep obscurity,
All that the heavens contain remain concealed,
For good so great as this,
No pain, however sharp,
Can be accounted worthy of the cost.
      That Good to which through blindness you are led,
Should make appear all other-having, Tile,
And every torment be as pleasure held,
Who, hoping to behold
Graces unique and rare,
May hold in high disdain all other lights.
      Ah, weary ones! Too long, too long our limbs
Have wandered o'er the terrene globe,
So that to us it seems
As if the shrewd wild beast,
With false and flattering hopes,
Our bosoms has encumbered with her wiles.
      Wretched henceforth, we see, though late, the witch
Concerned to keep us all with promises
(And for our greater hurt), at bay;
For surely she believes
No woman can be found
Beneath the roof of heaven so dowered as she.

Now that we know that every hope is vain,
We yield to destiny and are content,
Nor will withdraw from all our strivings sore;
And staying not our steps,
Though trembling, tired and vexed,
We languish through the days that yet are ours.
    Oh graceful nymphs, that on the grassy banks
Of gentle Thames do make your home,
Do not disdain, ye beauteous ones,
To try, although in vain,
With those white hands of yours
To uncover that which in our urn is hid.
    Who knows? perchance it may be on these shores,
Where, with the Nereias, maybe seen
'The rapid torrent from below ascend
And wind again
Back to its source,
That heaven has destined there she shall be found.

    One of the nymphs took the urn in her hand, and without trying to do more offered it to one at a time, but not one was found who dared. to be the first to try (to open it), but all by common consent, after simply looking at it, referred and proposed it with respect and reverence to one alone; who, finally not so much to exhibit her own glory as to succour those unhappy ones, and while in a sort of doubt, the urn opened as it were spontaneously of itself. But what shall I say to you of the applause of the nymphs? How can you imagine that I can express, the extreme joy of the nine blind men, where, hearing that the urn was open, they felt themselves sprinkled with the desired waters, they opened their eyes and saw the two suns, and felt they had gained a double happiness; one, the having recovered the light they had lost, the other that of the newly discovered light which alone could show them the image of the highest good upon earth. How, I say, can you expect me to describe the joy and exulting merriment of voices of spirit and of body which they themselves all together could not express? For a time it was like seeing so many furious bacchanals, inebriated with that which they saw so plainly, until at last, the impetus of their fury being somewhat calmed, they put themselves, in a row.

    73. *The first played the guitar and sang the following*:
    Oh cliffs, oh deeps, oh thorns, oh snap, oh stones,
Oh mounts, oh plains, oh valleys, rivers, seas,
How dear and sweet you show yourselves,
For by your aid and favour,
To us the sky's unveiled.
Oh fortunate and well-directed steps,
    The second with the mandoline played and sang:
    Oh fortunate and well-directed steps,
Oh goddess Circe, oh transcendent woes,
With which ye did afflict us months and years;
They were the grace of heaven,
For such an end as this,
After such weariness and such distress.
    The third with the lyre played and sang:
    After such weariness and such distress;
If such a port the tempests have prescribed,
Then is there nothing more that we can do,
But render thanks to heaven,
Who closely veiled our eyes,
And. pierced anon with such a light as this.
    The fourth with the viola sang:
    And pierced anon with such a light as this;
Blindness worth more than every other sight,
Pains sweeter far than other pleasures are,
For to the fairest light
Thou art thyself a guide,
Show to the soul all lower things are null.
    The fifth with the Spanish drum sang:
    Showing the soul all lower things are null,
Seasoning with hope the high thought of the mind,
Was one who pushed us to the only path,
And so did show us plain,
The fairest work of God,
Thus does a fate benign present itself.
    The sixth with a lute sang:

Thus does a fate benign present itself,
Who wills not that to good, good should succeed,
Or pain forerunner be of pain,
But turning round, the wheel,
Now rising, now depressed,
As day and night succeed alternately.
The seventh with the Irish harp:
As day and night succeed alternately;
While the great mantle of the lights of night,
Blanches the chariot of diurnal flames,
As He who governs all,
With everlasting laws,
Puts down the high and raises up the low.
The eighth with the violin:
Puts down the high and raises up the low,
He Who the infinite machine sustains,
With swiftness, with the medium or with slow,
Apportioning the turning
Of this gigantic mass,
The hidden is unveiled and open stands.
The ninth with the rebeek:
Re hidden is unveiled and, open stands,
Therefore deny not, but admit the triumph,
Incomparable end of all the pains
Of field and mount,
Of pools and streams and seas,
Of cliffs and deeps, of thorns and snags and stones.

After each one in this way, singly, playing his instrument, had sung his sistine, they danced altogether in a circle and sang together in praise of the one Nymph with the softest accents a song which I am not sure whether I can call to memory.

GIU. I pray yon, my sister, do not fail to let me hear so much of it as you can remember I

LAO.

74. *Song of the Illuminati*:
"I envy not oh Jove, the firmament,"
Said Father Ocean, with the haughty brow:

"For that I am content
With that which my own empire gives to me."
    Then answered Jove, "What arrogance is thine.
What to thy riches have been added now,
Oh god of the mad waves,
To make thy foolish boasting rise so high?"
    "Thou hast," said the sea-god, "in thy command,
The flaming sky, where is the burning zone,
In which the heavenly host
Of stars and planets stand within thy sight.
    "Of these, the world looks most upon the sun,
Which, let me tell you, shineth not so bright,
As she who makes of me,
The god most glorious of the mighty whole.
    "And I contain within my bosom vast,
With other lands, that, where the happy Thames
Goes gliding gaily on,
Which has of graceful nymphs a lovely throng.
    "There will be found 'mongst those where all are fair,
Will make thee lover more of sea than sky,
Oh Jove, High Thunderer!
Whose sun shines pale beside the starry night."
    Then answered Jove, "God of the billowy sea!
That one should ere be found more blest then I
Fate nevermore permits,
My treasures with thine own run parallel.
    The sun is equal to thy chiefest nymph,
By virtue of the everlasting laws,
And pauses alternating,
Amongst my stars she's equal to the sun."
    I believe that I have recalled it entirely.
    GIU. You can see that no sentence is wanting to the perfecting of the proposition, nor rhyme to the completion of the stanzas. Now if I by the grace of heaven have received beauty, a greater favour I consider is mine, in that whatever beauty I may have had it has been in a certain way instrumental in causing that Divine and only one to be found. I thank the gods, because in that time, when I was so tender (verde), that the amorous flames could not be lighted in my

breast, by reason of my intractability, such simple and innocent cruelty was used in order to yield more graces to my lovers than otherwise it would have been possible for them to obtain, through any kindness of mine however great.

LAO. As to the souls of those lovers, I assure you that as they are not ungrateful to the sorceress Circe for their blindness, grievous thoughts, and bitter trials, by means of which they have reached so great a good, so they can be no less grateful to thee.

GIU. So I desire and hope.

www.ingramcontent.com/pod-product-compliance
Lightning Source LLC
Chambersburg PA
CBHW071203160426
43196CB00011B/2186